"Insightful advice for all moms ⌐
be perfect, and this book remin
accomplishing so much on a da
-Je ⌐⌐⌐⌐⌐⌐, Actor on *Workin' Moms*
@jessalynwanlim

"I found reading this book SO helpful. There's no manual for being a mom in 2020, with the obligations of owning a business or for any mom who works really, there's a lot of guilt and exhaustion. I especially enjoyed the chapters on 'Mindful Parenting' with the discussion around raising whole kids so we avoid broken adults, that hit home for me! I want to raise whole kids!"
-Niki Papaioannou, Publicist, Business Owner
@nikiincto | www.nikiinc.ca

"A wonderful grouping of personal essays by fellow working moms, *Mama's Gotta Work* has a positive and encouraging message for women returning to the workforce after babies—and for those who never left. A must-read for all moms!"
- Shelley Ross, Mother of two
Owner of The Qualicum Toy Shop
www.qualicumtoyshop.com

"I wish there was a book like this around when I had my two boys. It is so important that women support each other and share their stories so that we can parent without guilt, and be open to how others choose to parent. There isn't a 'one fits all' approach to being a mom. It is personal, and I love that this book shares different stories and approaches to being a working mama. So much respect and love for the women in these pages."
-Helen Tansey, Photographer
www.SundariPhotography.com

"*Mama's Gotta Work* is a must-read for all working moms. This book has heartfelt, inspiring stories with practical knowledge and tools that will help you overcome the challenges of a busy schedule, manage mom-guilt, and find the emotional strength we have to acquire so we can be the best version of ourselves for our kids while we kick ass in our careers. Reading this book helped validate the feelings I've had for years, and made me feel less alone in my struggle with managing my career and being a present and conscious parent for my daughter. This book gives me hope that mother's will rise, feel empowered, and overcome any obstacle that is placed in front of them."

-Christina Whiteley, Speaker, Author, Social Marketing Expert
@thechristinawhiteley | www.ChristinaWhiteley.com

"They say 'life doesn't come with a manual—it comes with mother' . . . well *Mama's Gotta Work!* is pretty darn close to being that manual. It is a refreshing take on the narrative joys, responsibility, selflessness, and 'am I doing this right?' that comes with being part of the most fulfilling, important, and transformative club in the world—Motherhood."

-Stacy-Ann Buchanan
Actress, Filmmaker, TEDx Speaker, Mental Health Advocate
www.stacyannbuchanan.com | IG: @stacyannbuchanan

"*Mama's Gotta Work* is a must have for your bookshelf! Right from the intro, I knew this would be a book that will unite mama's together to share in the joys, sadness, milestones, and hardships of being a Mama. Many of my friends refer to me as 'Supermom,' so I especially resonated with Chapter Four: How Super Moms Really Do It All! Do yourself a favor and grab yourself a copy of this book. It will bring you through all the emotions, and give you a few Mom hacks to add to your tool box!"

-Steph Clark
Makeup Artist, Personal Branding Coach, Author
IG @stephkmua | FB @justwearthelipstick

Foreword by Catherine Reitman
Creator and Star of *Workin' Moms*

mama's Gotta Work!

Stories and Survival Hacks from Real-Life
Working Moms on Conscious Parenting,
Career Success, and True Fulfillment

Co-Authored By:
Krysta Lee I Amanda Drexler I Andie Mack I Charleyne Oulton
Domenica Orlando I Elizabeth Meekes I Erin Montgomery
Laura Morris I Lisa Evans I Marcia Miatke I Mary Ann Masesar Blair
Melissa Killeleagh I Michelle Emmick I Nanci Lozano I Pina Crispo
Sally Lovelock I Sharlene Rochard I Sharon Hughes-Geekie
Stephanie Card I Teresa Nocita

Contents

True Fulfillment: Trials and Triumphs

Survival Guide: Mom-Hacks 101

Foreword

Catherine Reitman
Creator and Star of *Workin' Moms*

Books about parenting generally scare me. Too often they are written by someone who doesn't know you, yet is demanding you to hit milestones that don't work for you or your child. However, in this case I know one of the writers. And she's the real deal. While Krysta Lee has been my stand in on *Workin' Moms* for over four years now, she has spiritually been so much more. Krysta is a workhorse. She managed to have two babies during the course of filming our series, and when she wasn't pregnant with these babies—she was pumping for them! And let me tell you that pumping on set is no luxury. Whatever romantic notion you have of being pregnant or a new mother while filming? Yeah, throw it away. Being a working mother in show business is grueling, and emotionally and physically taxing. So when Krysta approached me to write a foreword for this book, it was a no-brainer. Who better to speak to the real-life hardships and wins of being a working parent than Krysta?!

Anyone who knows Krysta can attest that her work ethic is only rivaled by her pure, unadulterated enthusiasm (I'm talking grade A, Disney-level positivity). I believe this comes from the gratitude I've witnessed from her. She believes, sincerely, that managing all of these complicated and challenging elements in her life is, in fact, a gift. This shift in mindset of being thankful had a massive impact on me. There have been so many days that I drove to set, filled with anxiety about this or that, and arrived to find Krysta—her face beaming joy and gratitude back at me. Krysta has been my gratitude North Star for four years and counting and it is my hope that this book will do the same for you. Now, if this level of gratitude and enthusiasm seems out of reach for you, I assure you that what you will find in these pages is that Krysta's joy and love of having it all, is truly contagious. The many days her children and husband would visit her on set, I was able to witness the level of commitment this woman applies to all that she does.

What I value in this book, from these writers, is the idea that being a working parent doesn't have to look a certain way. It must fit you. Maybe for you, working twelve to fourteen hour days, while pumping, isn't the right fit. For many it wouldn't be. However, the beauty of this book is Krysta and the others' ability to articulate what worked for them. So often, being a parent can feel like a marathon where you are in dead last, unable to see your fellow runners. This book feels like an invitation to see how other mothers train, run, and finish their races.

Dearest Mama,

Welcome! As you embark on your journey back to work after having your babes, we want to extend our open arms to embrace you into the incredible community of working mamas. The path that lies ahead may not always be an easy one, and that's okay.

There is an exceptional tribe of women here—and we have come together to support you, and share with you our most valued pearls of wisdom on the topics of conscious parenting, career success, and true fulfillment—with a super-sized dose of mom-hacks, too!

The idea came from a desire to have many working mamas' questions gathered into one space, so moms didn't have to look far for answers. The name of this baby birthed itself, time and time again, as we found ourselves saying to our kiddos, *"Mama's Gotta Work!"*

Whether you're returning back to work because you choose to, or because you have to, we are pleased to inform you: you're *never* alone. You have access to a school-bus load of mamas within the pages of this book, and can reference many different scenarios that may occur for you as well.

*This collection of stories from working mamas from all around the globe has been carefully crafted to encourage, inspire, uplift, and move you in ways with **all** the feels.*

Moms do so much for others, and no matter what your specific background, profession, age, stage, race, religion, or social status is— we want you to know that you are deserving of everything you desire, and you have the power within you to achieve anything you wish!

From the trials to the triumphs, to the ups and the downs, and all throughout the in-betweenie-weenies, we've *got* you! We have a wide range of expertise to share, with plenty of different family dynamics, and fifty (yes, fifty!) children combined.

From millennial-mamas to moms with decades of experience, here you'll receive insight from mompreneurs and small business owners, coaches of all kinds, artists, teachers, office administrators, law enforcement and healthcare professionals, actors, journalists, consultants, managers, shift-workers, models, personal trainers, podcast hosts, volunteers, studio directors and singers, and even our very own travel agent extraordinaire!

Be prepared to love on, learn from, laugh with, and be inspired by twenty every-day working mamas through their witty and unique perspectives.

Most of these mamas simultaneously wear several different career hats in addition to mom-ing, and the variety of experiences you'll read about within their chapters will cover dozens of scenarios—some of which may even surprise you, as you learn what many women go through after returning back to work post babes.

Whatever your current situation may be, you can take comfort in knowing this is a safe place to lean into—a judgement-free zone—full of like-minded MILFs (Moms I'd Like to Friend), who are open and willing to share as much as possible to help pave the path for you. We *get* it, and we have genuine understanding and empathy for mamas, especially when they've gotta work.

Take some time for you, today . . . Pour yourself a hot cup of coffee or tea (wine? You *go,* girl!). Grab a snack or three, cozy up in your favorite comfy clothes, then sit back and relax with *this* baby in your hands.

Allow us to entertain your mind and ease your thoughts for just a little while, with a light-hearted look into the lives of other fellow working mamas. We came, we saw, and we conjured-up a tell-all tale of real-life bits for you to read. Prepare to laugh, cry, contemplate, and hopefully learn a full-diaper load, too.

This is officially part of your go-to working-mama toolkit, with plenty of helpful hints readily available at your fingertips. Get your markers ready to highlight whatever resonates most with you!

As we put it all out on the table, rest assured there will be no milk left unspilled.

-Krysta Lee xox

Section One

Conscious Parenting: Mindful Mama

FEATURING:

Marcia Miatke
Sharon Hughes-Geekie
Sally Lovelock
Mary Ann Masesar Blair
Krysta Lee

Chapter One

The Conscious Working Mom

"May we put more emphasis on raising whole children, so we need less energy to heal broken adults."

Marcia Miatke

MARCIA MIATKE

www.marciamiatke.com
ig: @marciamiatke | fb:@marciamiatke
fbg: @empoweringwomenforsuccess
li: @marciamiatke | t: @marciamiatke

Marcia Miatke

Marcia Miatke is a leadership and emotional intelligence consultant, executive coach, international best-selling author, host of *The Hustler's Guide To Flow* podcast, female empowerment enthusiast, and conscious mother of two. Marcia transformed her life to overcome adversity (i.e., being born into poverty, adoption, and drug addiction) to build her career and business while nurturing her love and family life. Marcia is certified in Leading with Emotional Intelligence, and was awarded a full academic scholarship to complete her doctorate, and has research experience in leadership, emotional intelligence, and change. She was awarded the Zonta International Women in Business Scholarship and is a fully certified Law of Attraction coach.

Her mission is to empower others to lead exceptional lives by healing emotional wounds and building their emotional intelligence and resilience to experience more love, success, and fulfilment.

There we sat on the bathroom floor, both sobbing. An overwhelming feeling of guilt washed over me as I held her trembling body. Tears of regret streamed down my face for losing my temper just minutes prior. As I dried her little body, a flurry of emotions overcame me, a deep sense of love for this beautiful little soul, and layers of guilt that had nothing to do with the current situation. Losing my cool in that moment only compounded the lingering guilt I felt for separating from her father, for not providing for her in the way he could, for the time away from her as a working mom, and for not being the mom she deserved during our limited time together. I felt guilty about it all.

Looking into her tear-filled almond-shaped eyes, I apologized. I told her mommy was wrong to yell. I explained that even when mommy is angry, mommy never stops loving her; and that she deserves to be treated with love *all* the time, not only when she is *good*. She hugged me as if to say she forgave me, but the feeling of guilt that I was failing her as a mom remained.

WHY OUR CHILDREN TRIGGER US

Who would have thought our adorable little humans not only possess, but frequently exercise the ability to make us feel powerless, incompetent, and speaking from personal experience, literally bring us to our knees? Yet, that is why our children came into our lives. A child's presence and refusal to conform to the world around them pushes us in the most uncomfortable way to grow, to evolve, and to heal. Children by nature are chaotic and disorderly, which threatens the structure we grownups have put in place to make us feel in control or *safe*.

The inconvenient truth that many parents don't want to acknowledge, *"We are triggered not by their behavior, but by our own unresolved emotional issues"* -Dr. Shefali. Our child's behavior or perceived misbehavior brings to the surface unhealed, unprocessed or unintegrated emotional trauma.

Let's apply this to the shower showdown I experienced with my then two-year-old. The frustration and anger I felt was not the result of my daughter screaming in refusal to have her hair washed; even though that's what it felt like in that moment. I lost my temper because her defiance triggered a dormant feeling of not being in control, and as someone who likes to be in control, this was a threatening situation (to my ego).

THE CHILD WITHIN THE PARENT

Contrary to what we may think, when we are triggered as parents, we don't respond the way we would imagine an evolved adult would. We often respond the way a frightened or threatened child might. That's because within every adult is a child version of themselves who comes to the surface when an experience in their present life reminds them of a painful childhood experience. Many adults are unaware of the existence of their inner child and are therefore unaware of when they are responding from their child perspective. That's why many parents believe their anger in the moment is in response to their child's misbehavior and not something deeper within themselves. When a parent—unaware of their inner child—lashes out or loses their temper, much like I did with Aliyah, they may become resentful towards themselves or their child. Some parents may feel embarrassed and recognize that their response was *out of character*, but will not make the connection between the triggered emotion and a past emotional wound. Without first the awareness of the wounding and subsequent triggers, it is hard for a parent to truly be there for their child during emotionally charged situations.

For instance, if I was aware of how I was being triggered in the moment, I could have diffused the situation. I could have paused. Pausing could have allowed me to observe the way in which the emotions of fear and loss of control surged through my body. Becoming the observer, rather than the victim of my emotions, would have allowed me to respond as a loving and present mother, rather than a frantic and fearful one. I could have held space, remained calm, and made her feel loved rather than escalating the situation. I didn't respond as her loving mother in that moment because the frightened little girl inside me was doing her best to regain control of a threatening situation.

CONSCIOUS WORKING MOM HACK ONE: GAIN CLARITY AND CREATE SPACE

While working moms don't need another thing added to the laundry list of things we already do, understanding our emotions and triggers dramatically improves our relationships, especially with our little ones. Next time you feel triggered by your child (or anyone for that matter), ask yourself: *What unpleasant emotion am I feeling now?*

Don't judge the emotion or yourself for having it. Again, allow yourself to be the observer. Then, ask yourself: *What negative childhood experience is this reminding me of?* All of our unpleasant feeling emotions stem from somewhere; usually in childhood. Labeling the emotion and then finding a childhood example of when you felt like this, helps to recognize why this particular instance has triggered you. In the context of the childhood experience, ask yourself: *What was I most afraid of in that moment?*

Being aware of our emotions at that exact time helps us to be less caught up in the heat of the moment. Creating a few seconds' space between stimulus and response is game changing, especially in the parenting game. Oftentimes a couple seconds of presence is the difference between responding intentionally and reacting uncontrollably.

ACKNOWLEDGING THE CHILD WITHIN

As I noted, within each adult exists an inner child, a child version of themselves who still needs to be affirmed, told they're loved, they're safe, that it wasn't their fault, and that they're good enough just as they are. As parents, our inner child is the first we should be parenting and the one we'll continue parenting long after our children are grown. When our inner child feels neglected we are more likely to clash with our biological child. When our inner child does not feel loved (i.e., when we do not fully accept and love ourselves), it is impossible to love the child in front of us. We cannot genuinely love another unless we first love ourselves because we cannot give to another what we do not first have for ourselves. Most parents want to raise highly evolved children, yet have not done the work themselves to become highly evolved. Healing and tending to the child within us is a necessary step to our evolution and we can begin by simply checking in with her on a daily basis.

CONSCIOUS WORKING MOM HACK TWO: CHECK-IN WITH YOUR INNER CHILD

If you wake up feeling *off*, low energy, or in a mood you don't wish to continue your day with, take a moment to check in with your inner child. Ask her if she knows what's causing her to feel this way? She may say she's nervous about something at work. Then dig deeper to understand her perspective better: *What specifically are you nervous about?* Allow her to express and feel heard, then offer her support. *What will, or how can I make you feel a bit more at ease? How can I make you feel safe and supported in this moment?* She may need to be affirmed, or reassured or she may need some action to be taken. Whatever self-care she needs, do your best to give it to her. If she needs to feel supported and that she is not alone, you can remind her: *We're in this together and I'm here supporting, guiding and loving you.*

HEALING THE CHILD WITHIN US

Earlier I explained that our children have a way of triggering our unhealed pain. There is much we can discuss in regards to healing past trauma, but making your inner child feel loved is a great place to start. We can do this as affirmations in the morning before getting out of bed, in front of the mirror, or sporadically throughout the day. It's important to visualise your inner child when talking to her. I recommend looking at a childhood picture of yourself and speaking to yourself the way you would a small child. The following are ten statements your inner child needs to hear regularly.

Ten things you can say to your inner child:

1. *You are enough.*
2. *You are safe.*
3. *You are worthy.*
4. *You have the power to create your life experience.*
5. *You live in a new reality now.*
6. *It wasn't your fault.*
7. *I see you and love you.*
8. *I understand.*
9. *I forgive you.*
10. *I am here to guide and support you.*

Something as simple as regularly speaking loving words to our inner child can be transformational to our lives. And truly, until we do the work to nurture our inner child we will continue to perpetuate the pain we felt as children. We often see pain being passed down from one generation to another because in the same way that energy can never be destroyed, it can only be transformed; pain that is not transformed can only be transmitted. What I mean by that is if I am holding on to pain from a traumatic experience, I am likely to unintentionally project that on to my children. Then, if our children do not process or heal this pain in themselves, they too will pass it on to their children; and the cycle continues. With awareness of how we transmit our pain (i.e., low vibrating emotions), we can begin to stop the cycle of trauma. I believe that when you heal the mother, you heal the world because the mom is often the central figure in their children's lives.

CONSCIOUS WORKING MOM HACK THREE: AFFIRM YOUR CHILD

It is both empowering and terrifying to know the words we speak to our children become their inner dialogue for the rest of their lives. I invite you to take a moment to reflect on the inner dialogue you are creating for your child. After deciding I wanted to create an empowering inner dialogue for my daughter, I thought about the things I wished to hear most as a child. As often as I can I weave these affirmations into our conversations. What did you wish your parents said to you? What did you most need to hear? If you're unsure of where to start, refer back to the ten things to say to your inner child and begin saying them to your children.

MAKING YOUR CHILD FEEL SAFE

Most parents intend on being the best parents they can be. We do our best to give our children childhoods they don't need healing from, but in reality, regardless of how much healing we do, and how much we try not to project our pain on our children, we will react, lash out, and fumble repeatedly. Our shortcomings as parents, as well as other experiences outside the home, will wound our little humans. They will have their share of soul searching, deconstructing, and healing to do regardless of our level of vigilance in protecting them. After all, we can't prevent our children from being hurt, nor should we want to. Pain is a natural part of this human experience and an important part of their evolution. Our job as parents is to be their safe haven.

CONSCIOUS WORKING MOM HACK FOUR: ALLOW PAIN

Oftentimes we suffer as parents because we are unable to watch our children experience pain. We want to fix things, protect, and save them from discomfort. This again is a reflection of our unprocessed pain. Wanting to shield our children from pain signifies our unhealthy relationship with pain. Pain, or unpleasant feeling emotions are not something to eliminate, but rather something to move through. So the idea is not to shield our children from pain, but to help them have a healthy relationship with it. Here's how we can support our children during a painful experience:

- Be their safe place when they experience pain. This means allow them to share with you without the need to judge them or the situation.
- Apologise when we are a source of their pain. This is different to admitting I am wrong and you are right. This is you as their mother saying, "I'm sorry that I have caused you pain."
- Help them to *be* with the pain. Helping your child *be* with their pain means not distracting or helping them run from their pain.
- Help them process their pain. Help your child make sense of what they're feeling. Help them work through the pain so they can release it.
- Lead by example in processing and healing your pain. Encouraging your child process their emotions, but not processing your own is inauthentic. Our children follow what we do not what we say.

BEING A CONSCIOUS WORKING MOM

As if being a working mom isn't hard enough, why am I advocating we be *conscious* working moms? Let's take a few steps back and get some clarity on the conscious part. Consciousness is the state of being aware of and responsive to one's surroundings. Conscious parenting could be viewed as being aware and responsive to our child in the present moment. It's simple in theory (i.e., to be aware and respond), but most moms can admit that we're often not fully aware or responsive. Doing so requires us as mamas to be fully present. Being fully present with our child when there is a pile of emails we need to get through before bedtime can be difficult. Being fully present with our child when we have a presentation in the morning we don't feel prepared for can be stressful. Being fully present with our child when we're worried about our mother in a nursing home can be overwhelming. There is much in our current reality that preoccupies our minds and hinders our presence not to mention our past trauma and unprocessed emotions. There are layers of unprocessed emotions (often from childhood) that get in the way of being fully present with our children.

It is hard to be present. It's hard, and it's also necessary. Being a conscious working mom means we're willing to process our emotions. It means we're willing to look at our childhood wounds and work to process or transform the pain. It means not bringing emotional debris from our past into our blossoming relationship with our children. It means responding to our children as evolved and empowered women and not as wounded young girls.

Being a conscious parent is fundamentally different to traditional parenting, which asks *What on the outside needs to change to make me feel better?* while conscious parenting asks *Why am I being triggered by this behavior?* Conventional parenting seeks to correct the behavior of the child while conscious parenting seeks to heal the wounds within the parent. Contrary to popular belief it's not our job as parents to correct or discipline our child's behavior, but rather to ask what trauma, insecurity, fear, or unconscious anger their behavior is bringing to the surface. I acknowledge this is hard to do in the heat of the moment, but like most things, it becomes easier with practice.

WORKING MOM GUILT

That guilt that washed over me when I screamed at my toddler may sound familiar. The term *mom guilt* is as common as *play group* among mamas because not one of us is spared the sinking feeling of guilt. *Working mom guilt* is mom guilt on steroids. In addition to feeling day-to-day mom guilt, working moms feel guilty for not being traditional stay-at-home moms that do finger painting, morning play dates, and mommy and me yoga. I know I experienced, and sometimes still do, my share of mom guilt, especially for spending less time with my kids than stay-at-home moms.

From a conscious parenting perspective however, working moms shouldn't experience a higher degree of guilt. As conscious parents, the greatest gift we can give our children is presence—not to be confused with the amount of time spent with them. Working moms are just as capable of processing their emotions, being aware of and responding to their children in the present moment. That's right, working moms are no less capable of being conscious moms than stay-at-home moms.

USEFUL GUILT

Guilt is often described as a negative emotion, and one we should avoid feeling. By making ourselves wrong for feeling this emotion, we often get into a disempowering cycle of feeling guilty for feeling guilty. What if we reframed guilt into something useful? To do that, we need to establish that no emotion is either good or bad, negative or positive. All emotions, unpleasant ones included serve a purpose. Let's revisit the hair washing fiasco. Feeling guilty for losing my temper on my daughter signaled to me that:

1. I love my daughter deeply otherwise I would not have felt guilty, and;
2. How I reacted is not how I want to show up as a mother.

Guilt in small doses can inspire us to become better moms because without the uncomfortable feeling we may not be sufficiently motivated to change. For instance, it helped me identify and set the intention for how I want to respond in the future. Regardless of what we feel guilty for, let's allow the discomfort to fuel our desire to be the conscious mamas our children need us to be. To do that we need to identify how our childhood pain and trauma impacts our current reality and commit to doing the work to heal. Tending to and processing our own emotions is the first, and most critical step to raising whole, empowered and thriving children.

Chapter two

The Art of Guilt-Free Parenting

"As a mom, your goal is to provide your child with a strong foundation: a positive outlook; a love of learning; the life skills to be independent; the tenacity to be successful and the morals to be a good person. And then you watch, without judgement, as they build their life, knowing that the plan they follow will never be the one you had in mind."

Sharon Hughes-Geekie

SHARON HUGHES-GEEKIE

http://jumpstartcomm.ca
fb: @sharon.hughesgeekie
li: linkedin.com/in/sharon-hughes-geekie-82727417
t: @JumpstartAnd

Sharon Hughes-Geekie

Sharon Hughes-Geekie is a freelance writer and owner of Jump-Start Communications and Business Development. She resides with Winston, the giant wonder dog, in Kelowna, British Columbia. Mother of two grown children, Sharon has experienced the challenges and rewards of single parenting while juggling a career. Despite the inconvenience of diapers, drool, and daycare, she believes the working mama's challenges begin in earnest when a child can no longer be strapped into a car seat. Despite chaos and crisis on the home front, Sharon has mastered the art of appearing collected and capable in the boardroom—even while sporting mismatched shoes.

Sharon holds a Bachelor of Arts in Creative Writing from the University of Victoria.

The Art of Guilt-Free Parenting

Working mothers often say they feel guilty: guilty for going back to work, for putting their children in daycare and having them raised by strangers, for putting on a movie while they finish a project, or serving cereal for dinner because they forgot to buy groceries. Guilt is a feeling that you have done something wrong—something that goes against your moral code. As a working mother, I have experienced many emotions: fear, exhaustion, frustration, panic, joy, immense pride, and complete failure. No guilt.

I have two children that I raised as a single parent: my daughter Aly from age three and my son Davis from newborn. My children are now twenty-five and twenty-one respectively—technically adults. But being a mother, and a provider as it turns out, doesn't end when your children can legally drive, vote, drink, and smoke pot. When my children were young, I was a diaper-changer, homework helper, taxi driver, cheerleader, and chief cook in what felt like a twenty-four hour diner. As the mother of adult children, my role has evolved into banker, landlady, tax advisor and best of all, confidante.

Being a mother is not easy. Being a working mother requires the flexibility of a gymnast, the patience of a monk, the forgiveness of a saint, and the tenacity and resilience of a Jack Russell Terrier (but that's another story).

*The first step to becoming an effective,
guilt-free mama: developing self-awareness
and humility.*

TRY EVERYTHING. BE GOOD AT SOMETHING.

I know there are many things I am not good at: some because I lack knowledge or experience; others because I accept my deficiencies and am not motivated to overcome them. I do not swim well in deep water. I am not handy in the kitchen, though I did an amazing job of repairing the dishwasher with duct tape and Playdoh. I don't understand how my car works and I am not cut out to be a stay-at-home mom.

My daughter Aly was born when I was in my early thirties. I felt prepared. We had everything I thought we needed to be successful parents: established careers, life experience, a mortgage, money in the bank, plenty of love to give to a child, and a healthy dose of self-awareness. Although I desperately wanted children, I knew balancing work and motherhood was ultimately in the best interest of both me and my child.

Aly was a handful. She was just over two months old when I returned to work four days a week. She cried all night, every night and often for long stretches during the day. The doctor said it was colic and she would outgrow it. My tears on her first day of daycare were driven by fear and self-doubt. Could I function at work given my level of exhaustion, and was the person I employed to care for my child capable of handling her? As weeks turned into months, I was chronically late for work and when I did show up, my outfits were stained with freshly acquired spit-up. Fridays off were routinely spent sussing out new daycare arrangements.

I felt like a failure in life and my career, but I had chosen this path and was committed to making things work.

When Aly was five months old the all-night crying stopped. It was as sudden as turning off a light switch. I checked her crib regularly to make sure she was still alive. It took weeks before I accepted that four hours of uninterrupted sleep a night was a wonderful new reality. Based on the recommendation of a friend, I found an amazing day home that Aly loved and was close enough to my office that I could continue to breastfeed on my lunch break. I met other parents at the day home who felt as incompetent as I did. Armed with the knowledge that I was not alone, my confidence at work returned and I started to enjoy quality time with my daughter.

Once Aly reached the toddler stage, we spent my Fridays off at Parents and Tots: a program of crafts, stories, singing, and playtime. Most of the parents were the stay-at-home variety and this was just one of many organized activities they attended with their children. Parents exchanged program recommendations and phone numbers for future playdates—activities that occurred while my child was at daycare and I was at work. I struggled not to feel like the inferior outsider.

On one occasion, I watched as Aly and two little girls played house in a Playskool kitchen filled with miniature pots, pans, dishes, and plastic food. Aly was putting vegetables in a frying pan; the other little girls were putting a plastic chicken into the oven. "No," said Aly, pointing to the child-size microwave. "It goes in there." The girls looked puzzled. I suddenly realized that my daughter did not understand the purpose of an oven. In our home our quick, simple meals were cooked on the stove or warmed in the microwave. I was not even certain Aly realized that our oven door opened.

Similarly, crafts were also not my forte, and Aly and I frequently struggled through the creative portion of the program. One of the most memorable projects was a little sheep we constructed from a recycled candy tube, cardboard, cotton balls, and pipe cleaners. Once the project was complete, we looked around at the amazing creations of the other parent-tot teams. "Ours is kind of an ugly little sheep," observed Aly. "We aren't very good at this, are we?"

"Maybe not," I replied, "but we can't be good at *everything*." She looked doubtful, but for me, it was the birth of my new mantra: "*I have other skills!*" It was brilliant. Anytime I felt inadequate, I would reflect on those things I excelled at and would instantly feel better.

We tucked the little sheep into Aly's bag and joined the story circle. Aly was the only child who listened intently to the story—no squirming, talking, or poking the child beside her. After the story, parents stopped to compliment Aly on being so well-behaved. "You see," I said, "We may not be good at crafts but we both love stories and you are a great listener!" Aly looked pleased. As we headed to the car, Aly gave me a smug smile, pulled the ugly little sheep out of her bag and tossed it in the trash, content in the knowledge that she had other skills too.

LEADING BY EXAMPLE

Children learn by observing. A working mama lifestyle is an opportunity to help your child develop a good work ethic, learn about career options, and prepare for future employment. If you have a negative attitude about your job or call in sick because you feel like a day off, your child will model that behavior at school and later in life.

My mom was a stay-at-home mama; my dad was a petroleum engineer. That meant he worked in an office and didn't drive a train. Dad could best be described as stalwart. He was a loyal, conscientious employee who strove to get ahead. I only visited Dad's office once. When I was five, my brother was born. Dad took me to his work to hand out cigars and chocolates. I understood the secretaries typed and answered phones, but I had no idea what the men did. Years later I learned my dad played a key role in determining where the company drilled for oil.

By contrast, my children have had extensive exposure to my work. They knew from an early age that I was a writer, that I ran businesses, and helped other businesses be more successful. Whenever there was a staff birthday, the kids helped decorate that employee's office so they would arrive to a surprise on their birthday morning. They have distributed flyers at trade shows, sat through my speaking engagements and radio interviews, conducted market research at events, and stuffed envelopes. Just as we discussed school and after-school care over dinner, we also chatted at a high level about my day at work: things I had learned, projects I was working on, interesting people I had met. My kids understood that hard work and exceptional customer service were key to Mom bringing home a paycheck.

Volunteerism and having my kids involved in our active, rural community was also important to me. Barely school age, Aly and Davis served food and cleared tables at the community pancake breakfasts. I was a Sparks leader, Brownie leader, and coach for my son's indoor soccer team. I was on the executive for the Parent Advisory Council at their elementary school and on the Board for the community association.

*Our family had strong roots in the community
and our involvement with our neighbors
enriched our lives.*

It was the evening of Davis' grade five Christmas concert. The performance ended and I was helping to clean-up the auditorium. Davis was tired and grumpy, "Would it be humanly possible for us to attend a single event and not be the people putting away the chairs?"

"No, it wouldn't," I replied evenly. "We live in an amazing community because families like ours pitch in. If everyone does a little, no one is left doing a lot. The sooner you help, the sooner we go home." Off he stomped to do his part.

Fast forward to grade eleven: Davis invited me to the sports award banquet at his high school. As we walked into the gymnasium, his friends yelled at him to sit with them. Davis smiled and kept walking. "Go sit with your friends," I said. "I truly don't mind."

"No," Davis replied, "I invited you; I am going to sit with you." All night, I felt like a queen. He selected a table for us, brought me my food, and later went back to fetch dessert. After dinner, the awards began. Davis won Most Valuable Player for the track team, cross-country running team, and Athlete of the Year. My heart swelled. I didn't think it was possible to feel any greater pride for this wonderful young man I had raised on my own. The evening ended with the principal requesting everyone help with clean-up. The "cool" basketball players at the table behind us loudly announced they were having none of it and got up to leave. Davis rose, chair in hand and said, "Come on guys, let's put the chairs away. It won't take long." The group dutifully put down their belongings and picked up their chairs. I struggled to choke back tears. My once pouty nine-year-old was becoming a leader, an achievement as noteworthy as the awards he later displayed on his bedroom wall.

His success was my success: proof that, as a Mom, my guidance had made a difference.

BAD DAYS HAPPEN. STRIVE TO STAY POSITIVE.

The tween stage is the sweet spot between ages eight and thirteen when your children start to think and do for themselves. They are challenging boundaries, but have not yet arrived at the belief that you are actively trying to ruin their lives. As a parent, it is a time of transition. As your child's independence increases, your ability to keep them safe decreases. By eight they no longer require a car seat. By twelve they can stay home by themselves and are asking to date! Most importantly, this is the stage that hormones rage. Emotions run high and something seemingly insignificant can trigger a burning rage or flood of tears. This period in our little family was particularly volatile. By the time my son was eight, my daughter was twelve, and I was forty-five—well into menopause and on an emotional roller coaster of my own.

It was a Monday. Everyone was running late, including me. After a frantic search, I found my misplaced keys in the freezer where I had inadvertently dropped them while gathering ice packs for the kid's lunches. Davis had his nose in a book and Aly was *still* doing her hair. Unless she left now, she would miss the school bus. I reasoned, cajoled, pleaded. Finally! Aly snatched up her lunch, stuffed it into her knapsack, but before she could make a dramatic exit, Abby, our Jack Russell Terrier slipped between her legs and in seconds was running down the street. Aly looked back helplessly and quietly closed the door.

In those days we had two dogs: Abby, a canine Houdini, and Emma, a mixed-breed Shepherd. Davis offered to catch Abby but he needed to get to school. He darted out the door, and as he did, Emma pushed past him on a mission to retrieve Abby. Now both dogs were on the lam.

I was scheduled to give a presentation in less than an hour and felt ready to spontaneously combust. Dressed in a good suit, I threw on a pair of runners, grabbed a wiener from the refrigerator and went in search of the dogs. Emma was easy to retrieve. I escorted her home, grabbed a second wiener and went off in search of the elusive Abby. I found her two blocks away. I placed some wiener on the ground. She wiggled her little rump, swooped in and grabbed the meat before I could grab her. I tried again and again. I was almost out of wiener when a child caught Abby's attention. I dove at the dog, snatching her up in my arms and hanging on tight. She squirmed wildly but I succeeded in carrying her home. Back in the kitchen, there was a huge puddle of vomit. I had left the wieners on the counter and Emma had eaten them, package and all. Fighting back tears of frustration, I hastily cleaned up the mess, took a lint brush to my suit, replaced my runners with dress shoes and headed out the door.

I arrived at the venue ten minutes late, smelling like a hotdog. I was ready to put the insane events of the morning behind me, but as I climbed out of the car I realized I was wearing two distinctly different shoes. On the left foot, a navy shoe with a block-heel; on the right, a black patent pump. How could anyone not notice this? I felt like I had been sucker-punched. When my turn came to speak, I walked self-consciously to the front, contemplating what I should do. Had it been a room full of women, I would have joked about my crazy morning. Looking around at the suits and ties, I opted to hide my feet and took refuge behind the dais. The event ended with coffee and networking. Feeling brazen after a stellar presentation, I ventured into the open room, my shoes in full view. If anyone noticed, they had the good sense not to mention it to the menopausal Mama.

Bad days happen, and staying positive is a survival skill—a skill that becomes increasingly important as the tween years evolve into the tumultuous teens.

The teen years are arguably the hardest stage of parenting. As my children approached adulthood, I nostalgically longed for simpler times, like when dry Cheerios or Goldfish crackers could make a tearful child smile. Surviving the teen years requires compassion, compromise, restraint, thick skin, and a gym membership. Only through vigorous exercise can you generate enough happy hormones to keep you positive, and sane, until your children reach the magic age of twenty.

THERE ARE NO PERFECT PARENTS

We have all said it: "I will never be like my mother!" Sometimes negative learning is as effective as positive parenting. I am neither patient nor punctual—traits that continue to drive my children crazy. No surprise, they are both extremely patient and always on time.

Being a guilt-free mama is recognizing that there is no such thing as perfect parenting.

You do your best. You make mistakes, and if you are very lucky, your children grow into good, productive people that embody a few of your more positive attributes. As a single, working mama, my kids and I needed to be a team. Growing up, Aly and Davis were as accountable to one another as they were to me. Just as I have been there for the challenges, disappointments, successes, and celebrations in my children's lives, they have been there for mine. I look at my adult children—still very much works in progress—and I feel hopeful for their futures. It has not been an easy journey for our little family, but we have made some wonderful memories along the way. And at the end of the day, I have had an amazing career, and my kids turned out okay.

Chapter three

The Day I Walked Into a Child's Mental Health Center

"Stop looking for your individual unique child in a book, you will not find them there."

Sally Lovelock

SALLY LOVELOCK

www.althorpmontessorischool.com
ig: althorp_montessori_school | fb: @AlthorpMontessoriSchool

Sally Lovelock

Sally Lovelock found her passion while working at a Montessori school in a small village in Surrey, England. Her loyalty and passion for inspiring children to shine and adults to rise can be mistaken at times for a fiery side. Her goal is to reach as many early years educators and parents on the importance of the absorbent mind from birth to age six, and how we can guide these little leaders on a path to make a big impact on our Earth. Now living in the Niagara Region in Ontario, Canada, Sally credits her reiki certificate for helping her find inner peace and balance while juggling between her own Montessori school and two extraordinary boys.

The Day I Walked Into a Child's Mental Health Center

I am a natural caretaker and knew at the age of fifteen while taking a live-in nanny job that my direction in life involved children. Not knowing if that meant working with them, having my own, or perhaps becoming a midwife. If I was going to have children of my own, my life's master plan needed to come together; and that started back in a small village in Surrey, England at the age of twenty-one. After the beautiful three months I spent caring for my father there, I needed to connect with who I was and where I was going. I spent days sitting on a bench near my father's grave, and this healing time helped me discover that I had the ability inside to heal myself. As the anger of losing my father released, it opened up space within me to welcome spiritual cleansing. My world became so large and full of possibilities.

There it was in the paper in front of me, a job posting for a Montessori assistant at a local school nearby. I didn't know much about Montessori, but through years of nannying I knew I had enough experience with children to follow this next direction. So here I am young and full of confidence walking into the classroom! My first impression was, *what is going on in this classroom?! Surely this is some sort of boot camp or are these children actually robots?* It took me one week to know I had found my life's passion; Montessori offered these children freedom within a well-prepared calm and peaceful environment. The children had independence through purposeful work that came from the inner will. They were our guides, and we followed their lead.

I discovered that we must adapt to meet the needs of the child, the child must not be expected to adapt to our hectic world.

I later received my Casa International diploma in Montessori Pedagogy through London, England, and took the opportunity to open my own school in 2007 at the age of thirty-three. This opened the doors to more Montessori trained staff and gave us the opportunity to offer more children this approach to education. With many seminars, conferences, and workshops our knowledge grew, and we became more aware of the mental health of children today. We also learned that we too would continue to grow our knowledge and understanding of them as we continue to touch lives of individual unique children. This was when I discovered that I might be a control freak, but I prefer to describe myself as passionate! Growing our school meant delegating and handing over my power to other very capable montessorians. It also meant hiring staff that could live up to not only my expectations but also the expectations of the parents that had only known me as the teacher. I soon learned how to respond to parents when they said, "But we don't want someone else teaching our children, we want you!" Moving forward twelve years, they no longer ask for me: a win for my staff!

Life at this point seemed overwhelming as we grew, yet very well organized as I worked long hours, but little did I know that I was about to face my reality! Yes, it was time to think about babies of my own because that was the master plan. I was thirty-five years old and had enough preparation for this next step, right? My home was going to be the most peaceful environment offering my future babies a Montessori-from-birth experience. High five to all those Montessori moms out there that succeed on that goal!

My journey started with fertility issues. After many tests and no known discoveries as to why we could not fall pregnant I went through intrauterine insemination, and we were so thankful to conceive on the first try as we watched so many women struggle (may they all find peace). Most of us remember the *moment* we get pregnant; I sure do. This was the day I showed up late for our school trip! Well, I went to the clinic one hour after my husband and became pregnant without him even being there. It was funny, really. Conceiving without my husband present, mama has to work! I made it to the pumpkin patch that day unsure if that wagon ride would affect the outcome of whether or not I would conceive that day.

You announce your pregnancy, and that opens the doors for conversations and opinions that may not be welcomed. We find ourselves in many debates, nurse or bottle, circumcise or not, natural or drugs, home or hospital, midwife or doctor, crying it out or co-sleeping, the list goes on. But I think we can all agree that no matter how that baby comes into the world only we as the mother know the right answers to our questions. We judge too fast; we shame other moms, and through experience at my school I can honestly say this happens without even realizing it. No one wants to be *that parent*! Then there is religion and what school to send your child to. Like we didn't have enough pressure on us, the last thing we need is questioning ourselves based on decisions made by other mothers.

So where does this leave me? Working mom, running my own business, employees, students, and their parents. No maternity leave and a chronic migraine sufferer. I'm pretty sure this is called Superwoman, right? This was all part of my plan; this was my dream. Lying in the hospital after a cesarean section with a failed epidural, latching my baby, and trying to understand his vomiting. Yes, I was the one shooting milk in my baby's eye. Some moms wish to produce milk, however I walked around work with my staff telling me my boobs are leaking or that I had baby vomit on me. From the hospital I went straight back to my office, attachment parenting was the choice I made for my children. That meant sleepless nights with my baby sleeping on me until he was big enough to sleep beside me. Nursing on demand and sitting in my office with my baby asleep on me. The neck aches are still there ten years later. On the positive side, my children are both very secure and confident boys. With some separation setbacks for my youngest I knew there was a fine line in making sure they had their independence and *listening to their voice when they have an opinion.*

The struggle is real when balancing the job of two women; a working mom is still a full-time mom! I have had the joys of keeping my boys with me until the age of six. My children attended my school until they graduated and moved on to grade one. My staff and I will never forget that first day of school for my oldest son, as he stood on his school playground across the road from us, waving to us at recess. We all had tears coming down our faces. We were scolded for going over to the school gate by his teachers. My poor little guy cried himself to sleep that night, it didn't matter what I said or how tight I held him; he was inconsolable. He said I was the worst mom in the world for sending him to the worst school ever. This makes me laugh; I think he was pretty darn lucky to have his mummy across the street. It was such a privilege to not worry about childcare options. Oh wait, I'm still trying to figure out if that was a privilege because I remember pulling my hair out as my children followed me around at work.

Just when we finally get into a rhythm, back to work with a new schedule, along comes baby number two. Oh, the guilt, it's very real! I was lying in bed with my oldest son while he slept, I cried, I whispered in his ear how sorry I was that the very next day (a planned cesarean) I would be sharing my love with his brother. Then witnessing his rejection of his baby brother, why couldn't I have one of those easy transitions where the sibling is crying with joy? How long would it take? It was a quick five weeks before Leo would be feeding his baby brother Darcy and kissing him. Watching that sibling bond is worth every minute of the sibling fighting.

Oh, baby two, how you tested my energy! How did I make it to work each day? Toddler in tow and a baby on my breast every hour, twenty-four hours a day. The girls at work would ask me how many times I woke in the night. Just don't ask, this was my plan, I've got this. But the truth was, my staff had it. I had the support of staff that had become family. They took care of the business while my baby slept on his mummy.

As long as I had enough time to get payroll in and take tuition payments, we would keep on going! This is why delegating and letting go was key to professional and personal growth.

Recognizing that Superwoman is fiction; reality is: it takes a village to raise a child.

The most important part of growing my business and my family at the same time was consistency and order. *When meeting the needs of the children we are making life run smoothly.* These little people rely on us to prepare and organize. For me this meant quality staff and the freedom to have my baby in my arms. I had confidence in my people; I had confidence in myself; this is what respecting my children as little people looked like for me. I was able to recognize that although my career came before my babies, *I had to shift my mindset and recognize that my children came before my work.*

So, when did stress creep in and how did I overcome it? Well, as important as my children and work were, I knew that I was the glue that needed to hold it all together so that meant *me time!* Oh yes ladies, own those spa days! *Self-love is what you need to keep you motivated.* Find what it takes to bring you calm. You know yourself better than anyone. A gym routine and reiki is a must for me and when I can fit in a girl's night, walking amongst the trees or looking at the lake I'll put it in my schedule without guilt. I'm sure for some it will be that glass of wine and a bubble bath! There will be days when you can not fix your child's day and you will feel defeated, they will go through illness, bullying, and many failures.

Remind yourself that you need to find your way so you can be organic; sometimes just being present is the only answer.

So, what do I say to my boys when they tell me they will never forgive me, or they don't like me? *"Mum win for me!"* This is not what they want to hear at the time, and that kind of makes me smirk. I know that I am parenting when my children are angry at me, and that's okay! I also know that they respect me and that my guidance will offer them tools they will one day need. My advice based on experience is to do some research when making a life altering parenting decision. We often follow trends or follow the lead of other mothers. An example is letting your baby cry it out, look at the research of neuroscientists that have the studies to show exactly what is happening to your baby when they cry it out. My physical body will be forever sore for the ten years I co-slept with my babies, but our nights were peaceful and that provided them with a great start to the following day. As the years go by I have observed how easy my boys are when it comes to dentist visits, doctor appointments, and hospital visits. I believe without a shadow of a doubt that my decision to co-sleep with my children has built a strong sense of security in my relationship with my children and therefore meltdowns are not necessary. Just remember one thing: **stop looking for your unique individual child in a book, you will not find them there.**

Trust your own intuition, you know your child better than any doctor or teacher.

When I became a single mum, it was time to co-parent; we had a big shift in our home. The dynamics were changing, and this was scary for us all. My children had two homes, and that was not how I envisioned our future. This is when day by day was the only way. I got up for work, got my children to school, and went to bed. I really have no idea what happened throughout the day (I'm sure we ate and showered). The only thing I knew was that my hiring skills were on point because my mind was certainly not at the office even though my body was and somehow the school was smooth sailing. Guilt clouded my brain, it was just a ball of fog consuming me. Then came the day I cried like a child as I sat at the top of the stairs, all I could say to my children was "I'm sorry boys, your mummy is so lost." My oldest son said, "Mummy I have never seen you cry!" I had given my children the vision of working mum, powerful, strong and independent. They had not seen my ability to release such emotions or the benefits in doing so. I dropped my oldest child at school and let the principal know we had an emotional morning. My youngest went to my school as his godmother was also my right hand in the office. I cried all the way to a children's mental health center; it makes me laugh now. I walked in and told my story about breaking down in front of my children. The counselor looked at me and said, "*You are beautiful, your children are so lucky to have you.*" WAIT, WHAT?! I'm pretty sure I just told you I'm the worst mum in the world and my children need your help! I share this story openly because it helps us see that sometimes our own judgments on ourselves is our biggest mum failure. *We need to be open with others and keep our stories real.* Sometimes it will only take a simple statement or fact from another person to help us see that we are actually winning! *"YOU ARE BEAUTIFUL,"* so simple yet so powerful on that day.

When we have to choose between crying and laughing sometimes laughing is easier. My ex-husband is Catholic so after Montessori school my boys went to catholic school and this year is communion for my youngest. I had to take my son to church for preparation classes and the priest is at the front of the church talking about the sacrament of marriage. I'm sitting with some of the mums (all married), and felt so hurt that my children had to listen to the priest talking about their parent's divorce as a sin. I chose laughter, I turned and looked at the other ladies and said "well now he is just picking on me," we laughed. These are the moms that had my children over for playdates while we tried to keep as much *norm* in our children's lives through the separation. These are not the mums that gossiped behind our backs and decided to judge. They say you know who your friends are when you go through tough times, well divorce was the eye opener for me!

May we all have the support of other mums when we need to talk, from the ones who listen without judgment. One day we will find that the road we walk may be unclear, and we can't find the answers we need. Every one of us is living our own unique parenting journey. You may be a working mum, a stay-at-home mum, or sadly a hospital mum; but we all share strength. Give that gift to one another. *If you think you are the best mama, you probably aren't; if you think you are the worst mama, most likely you aren't; but you certainly are your child's everything.*

Chapter Four

How Super Moms *Really* Do It All!

"As the matriarch and leader of the family, we need to create an environment in which we can succeed, feel comfortable telling others what we need and accepting that help so we can do our jobs well."

Mary Ann Masesar Blair

MARY ANN MASESAR BLAIR

www.learngrowtransform.net
ig: @maryann.yourfitnessnurse | fb: @HigherLevelFitness
li: @maryann-yourfitnessnurse

Mary Ann Masesar Blair

Mary Ann's love for research, education, care coordination, and nursing entrepreneurship propelled her to seek roles where she could share her knowledge on how fitness, daily habits, and self care practices impact our health and happiness.

Raised a first generation Filipina in a neighborhood where she was exposed to many ethnicities, cultures, religions, and personalities, she learned that to master a new way to be, one must learn a new way to think. It's okay to challenge conventional ways of living. Not wanting to be bound to nursing and traditional ways of approaching health and fitness, she created her own role and is now Winnipeg's first and only Fitness Nurse.

Alongside her husband, they co-founded Higher Level Fitness with the mission to educate, empower and equip others with tools to self-create lifestyle health for optimal long-term wellness. It's been a rollercoaster of a ride with many stories to share, but for Mary Ann, becoming a mother has been the most challenging leadership role she's ever accepted, yet the most rewarding and fun-filled one to date.

When she can break free from mom and work duties, she is geeking-out with her husband on all things health, travel, and conscious living; alone meditating, journalling or reading non-fiction; walking out in nature soaking up enlightened conversations with her son; sweating in the gym or a hot yoga class; or at a local cafe sharing life with her favorite people.

WHO ARE *YOUR* SUPER MOM ROLE MODELS?

Our beliefs about motherhood and working come from our experiences as a child growing up. Through observation, imitation, and modelling, we learn how to respect ourselves and our time from our mothers, sisters, girlfriends, aunts, and grandmothers.

Culturally, two competing stories dominated my beliefs about motherhood and my decision to be a mom. You either focus on becoming successful in your career OR choose marriage, raise children, and be the happy housewife. There was no in-between option. I believed for a very long time that work could NOT be balanced with family life, and that ambition was incompatible with motherhood. So I delayed having children in favor of focusing on my career.

I am not alone in this decision.

Many Generation X and millennial women are opting to be child-free or deliberately delaying motherhood *by choice*. In one study by the Center for Work-Life in 2011, they found 43% of college educated, working Generation X women between the ages of thirty-three and forty-six are childless, even though three quarters of these women are in established relationships.[1]

Twenty-eight percent of Gen Xers worked ten hours more a week than they did five years prior, and a study by the Urban Institute reporting on the millennial generation during the years between 2007 and 2012 pointed out that birth rates among twenty-something women declined over fifteen percent![2]

---

1   Belkin, Lisa. "Do Gen X Women Choose Work Over Kids?" *New York Times* (blog), June 30, 2011, https://parenting.blogs.nytimes.com/2011/06/30/gen-x-women-choose-work-over-kids/
2   Newman, Susan. "Should We Worry About Millennials Not Having Babies?" *Psychology Today* (blog), April 25, 2018, https://www.psychologytoday.com/us/blog/singletons/201804/should-we-worry-about-millennials-not-having-babies

The message:
having children is a career obstacle.

Here's what I learned to believe from my childhood about mothering and working:

The role of spouse takes the backseat. Being a working mother meant that quality alone time with my significant other would decrease tremendously and the quality of the relationship would be at risk.

Time to plan, shop, travel, and advance in my career would be gone. The cost of raising a child in Canada can go up to $18,000 a year until the age of eighteen![3] I felt the deflating of my desired lifestyle to travel when I wanted, shopping with zero guilt, and opportunities of furthering my education got stronger every time I watched other moms say no to opportunities because they "had children now, that boat has sailed."

Household duties pile up, and overwhelm and frustration builds. Raising a family requires a division of housework, parenting duties, and financial obligations. My role models were the mom managers of their families. Appointments, clothes shopping, birthday parties, parent meetings, extra curricular activities, housekeeping, cleaning, and laundry often fell in the hands of the matriarch. What kind of life is this? I could barely manage myself!

Dividing attention between work and kids creates mom guilt. Having to leave your child with another caregiver when you have to work can get real emotional. As a child, I strongly remember those moments waving bye to my mom as she hopped on the bus to go to work, and crying until my caregiver would find something to distract me. I saw it when my best friend would drop her daughter with me to go to work and as much as she loved to be with me, she always asked why mom had to work and why couldn't she stay home and spend time with her? Separation anxiety is real!

Self care is last on the list of things to do. Ninety percent of mothers report taking better care of their families than they do of themselves, and a full twenty-five percent admit they haven't done anything just for themselves in more than a year![4] Straight madness!

---

3   Choi, Barry. "The Cost of Raising a Child in Canada," *Money We Have* (blog), September 23, 2019, https://www.moneywehave.com/the-cost-of-raising-a-child-in-canada/

4   Shulman, Joyce. "It's Time to Reject the Martyr Mom Syndrome," *Thrive Global* (blog), December 1, 2019, https://thriveglobal.com/stories/its-time-to-reject-the-martyr-mom-syndrome/

My mother worked two jobs for as long as I can remember, yet early in my life, I learned what she really wanted was a career in criminology. She was told by her father that a career in criminology was a "man's job" and that *her* role was to finish school, have children, and raise a family. So, right after she completed her business administration degree in the Philippines, she immigrated to Canada with her sister, and within that year, got married and gave birth to me—all by the age of twenty-three. I watched both my parents work in jobs that were not their first choice just to make ends meet. My dad worked the night shift in a machine factory and my mom worked the day shift in a nursing home. Time to play, dinners at the table, and one-on-one time with either parent felt non-existent. They were always working.

On the other hand, my grandparent's place was the after school daycare. I have many happy memories of walking to my grandparents with my classmates and spending a lot of time sitting in the kitchen asking my Lola questions while she prepared dinner and set up the table for all of us to eat. I remember her telling me that caring for children was her work, her service to God. She openly shared her love for my Lolo, made sure her outdoor garden and home were clean and attended to, she was also very active with the church and showed every child she cared for love and attention.

The world is so different now from what my parents and grandparents had grown up in. My mother's love was demonstrated in how she sacrificed her wants for my brother and I, and at the same time, my Lola's expression of love was the amazing feeling of seeing her doing what brought her pure joy. They were my super mama role models and their experiences shaped my beliefs of how to mother.

MY STORY OF SUPER MOM SYNDROME

Feeling unfulfilled as a clinical nurse educator and case management consultant, I switched career paths in my early thirties to pursue my passion in fitness, natural health, and holistic wellness. I left the corporate health care system in beautiful Vancouver, British Columbia, and with my then boyfriend, we packed it all up and moved back to be with family in our hometown Winnipeg, Manitoba.

He proposed to me on the drive home and within weeks before we settled in, we secured a location where we would build our dream together—a business to educate, empower and equip our community with the tools to learn, grow, and transform in their fitness and health care journey.

After fifteen years of working in jobs that were not bringing me fulfillment, I finally felt like I was on the right path, putting together my ideal career, where I could do meaningful work and open up opportunities to further invest in education, networking, and business entrepreneurship. We married a year later and within six months, I was pregnant with my son.

Entering motherhood is one of those memorable life events that have the power to alter our sense of self.

In other words, they can bring on a whole new level of crazy!

Super mom is defined in dictionary.com as "a mother who successfully manages a household and cares for her children while holding a job or being active in her community."

In today's age of social media, images of super moms are flashed in our faces on a constant basis.

The perfect furniture matching breastfeeding nursing pillow, soothing the angelic newborn; the maternal body bouncing quickly back to pre-baby body; and the put together mama, shopping the mall with a happy baby in tow. It all appears so easy to achieve. Yet, behind the highlight reels are overstuffed diaper bins, laundry everywhere, dishes piling up and—wait—*did the baby get their afternoon feeding yesterday? Did I feed with the left breast first or was it the right? I forgot to record the last time he pooped. Gawd! Why didn't hubby put the wet wipes back in the diaper bag? Shit, did I even brush my teeth this morning?*

Why we hide our struggles and imperfections like it is something to be ashamed of is *learned behavior.* Yet in the meantime, we mothers suffer in silence because we somehow believe we need to be super mom on our own or we fail. In pursuit of the images of perfection I had in my head, I constantly pushed myself to achieve the impossible.

Super mom syndrome is the delusional belief held by a mother that she can do all things for all the people in her life at all times, while perfectly managing herself. I was a classic case, experiencing the ABCDEF symptoms associated with super mom syndrome as per Dr. Demartini[5]:

- Anger and aggression.
- Blame and betrayal.
- Criticism and conflict.

---

5   Demartini, J. Supermom Syndrome - Symptoms and Treatment. Retrieved from https://drdemartini.com/supermom-syndrome/

- Depression and feeling down.
- Exhaustion and exit strategies.
- Frustration and fatigue.

Running a business and growing a family requires a significant amount of energy, structure, and organization, and I was failing. I needed to create a space for me to do what I believed would ultimately put all of us in a better position as a family and a small business or it was all going to fall apart.

In my desperation, I unravelled the polarizing beliefs I had about work and motherhood and how the two very limited, yet competing stories dominated the way I was living my life. You give life to what you give energy to and to live my days thinking that I could do it all by myself was completely draining my energy. I was trying to be both like my hard working mother and my always available Lola to my son. I was so determined to NOT be the mother who felt frustrated or resentful about the career dreams she gave up yet I was giving life to a dominant narrative that perpetuated and fulfilled itself.

Something had to shift.

I started placing my energy on finding different role models, real women who made their professional mark *after* children. I wanted to connect with the women who did NOT find their children to be an impediment to their professional success and career fulfillment. I wasn't seeing these stories in the media, but I knew they were out there. In finding these women and getting their stories, they would bring me a source of ideas, lessons and blueprints for creating my own version of personal and professional success.

THE SUPER MAMA SECRET: ASKING FOR AND ACCEPTING HELP

A story I was living behind was that if you can't figure everything out for yourself, you're telling others you're weak, lazy, ignorant, dependent, or incapable of doing your job. Whether it's personally or professionally—competent people do not ask for help. Besides, who has time to teach someone else how to do the work I do? Heck, I don't even have the money to hire out!

In Wayne Baker's book, *All You Have to Do Is Ask,*[6] he identifies reasons why we don't or won't ask for help:

---

6   Baker, Wayne. *All You Have to Do is Ask: How to Master the Most Important Skill for Success.* New York:Random House LLC, 2020.

- We underestimate other people's willingness and ability to help.
- We over-rely on self-reliance.
- We perceive there to be social costs of seeking help.
- We don't know what to request or how to request it.
- We fear seeming selfish.

Can you relate to some of these no good reasons to not ask for help? Check them off now and sit with those feelings.

Healthy lifestyle expert, successful business owner, and mother first, Chalene Johnson posted on her social media outlets that I tumbled upon, a question that would change the trajectory of how I would reinvent my super mama paradigm.

There is smart success and then there is stressed success. Don't you want to work less, make more money and reinvent the way you approach your family and work?

It takes a growth mindset to break up with the identity that *I should be able to do it all*, and side note: *should* is a low vibe word, get it out of your vocabulary right this instant!

Courageous confidence is the super mama power of knowing what you don't know and knowing when to ask.

As I started speaking to and spending time with this new kind of super mama, what they stated over and over again was that their key to success was asking for and accepting help from others. Asking for advice demonstrates confidence, conveys wisdom, and a strong understanding of self. By asking for help you know what action steps to take to reach the next level. By accepting help, you display compassion for self and service to others.

I started to believe that professional fulfillment and family *can* successfully coexist.

We routinely underestimate others' willingness and ability to help. We fear we'll be rejected. Or we figure that even if others are willing to help, no one will have the time or ability.

Give yourself the permission to ask for help. In doing so, we focus our energy, presence, and joy towards our passions that only free time can give us. When we outsource the help we need, we create opportunities for other people to shine in *their* passions. When we ask for and accept help from others, we build trust in ourselves *and* from those we are asking. We are using this time as an opportunity to invest in unique human resources, create a life we love, and for them to share their skills with us!

It takes a community to raise a child, and it starts first with the courage to ask for and accept help.

As the matriarch and leader of the family, we need to create an environment in which women can succeed and feel comfortable telling us what they need to do their jobs well. As mamas who gotta work, we have a responsibility to each other to be honest about the challenges we face and act as supporters in trying times. There's comfort in knowing that we're not alone and that other women in all likelihood are experiencing similar challenges.

LEADING BY EXAMPLE: WHERE CAN YOU ASK FOR MORE HELP?

In my work, I help busy professionals who are in a life transition (ie. pregnancy, perimenopause, new health diagnosis, motherhood), carve time to focus on their nutrition, fitness, and health. I help them examine their current lifestyle and then work together on creating a life they feel excited to live.

We must allow the time to mourn the end of the person we were, so we can shift into the person we can become. Time-track your life for seven days and expose the story of how you spend your choices. If we work forty hours and sleep fifty-six hours, that leaves us seventy-two hours a week for everything else that is important.

It's not about time management, it's about choice, how are you spending your choices? Consider how much your time is actually worth.

Can spending fifteen dollars an hour for your niece to take your vehicle for three hours each week to top up the gas, take it to the wash, and ensure regular maintenance be worth those three hours you would now use for one-on-one time with your child, to build your career, or finish a work project? Can you take advantage of your gym's two hour child-minding service or hire a housekeeper and use that time to study a skill you want to learn more about? Can you ask another mama to exchange time to help each other out? How much is your time worth?

Where can you ask for more help?

I invite you to connect with me and share your story. Professional fulfillment and family *can* successfully coexist. Let me HELP you align with your priorities, take conscious action towards your goals, and live your highest and best self. You got this!

Chapter Five

The Juggle Is Real!

"We must consciously recognize and honor what makes us feel good as individuals, as women with careers, and as mamas because that is how we truly become fulfilled."

Krysta Lee

KRYSTA LEE

www.KrystaLee.com
ig: @KrystaLee111 | fb: @Krysta.Lee.Fanpage
li: www.LinkedIn.com/In/KrystaLee
t: @Krysta_Lee | yt: www.YouTube.com/KrystaLee123
imdb: www.IMDB.me/KrystaLee

Krysta Lee

Krysta Lee is a singer and songwriter, actor, author, artist, coach, and health and wellness marketing executive who is the proud mama of two beautiful babes (Jaxon and Lillee), and wife to her twin flame, DJ. Her family (and faminals!) live a *modern-day-hippie* lifestyle in Prince Edward County, Ontario, Canada. She's an optimist, a goal-getter, and a big-dreamer who's had a passion for creative writing since her early childhood days.

Living her best life by the motto #SpreadLove, Krysta Lee is all about good vibes and positive energy. She loves her friends, family, fans, and all things animal related. She is a vegan, nature-loving yogi, guided by universal truth which she explores through meditation, channeling, and journaling. She thrives off of being in true states of happiness, health, success, and wealth; and prides herself on working hard (playing harder!), exercising regularly, and expressing gratitude daily.

Krysta is honored to be featured as a contributing author in this book, and is exceedingly grateful for the opportunity to be part of such an epic collective and movement, alongside such powerhouse women! Empowering mamas is very important to her because she believes that as women, we have an obligation to make a positive impact on the world. She understands that our future is a direct result of the actions we take today, and hopes to inspire as many people as possible with her life's work.

WHO (AND WHAT) IS A *WORKING MOM?*

A quick search revealed along the lines of the following definition: "Working Mothers are women who are mothers, and who work outside the home for income, in addition to the work they perform at home in raising their children." Okay. How many of y'all are applauding, and who's shaking their damn head, like, WTF?! *Right?!*

Defining a Working Mom is one of those grey areas—And I'll be damned if anyone thinks the above defines what I personally do as a working mother.

The title *working mom* insinuates infinite possibilities, because the most important word of the two is *mom*, and that itself is the ultimate full-time *job! Mom* is one of those all-encompassing titles, which contains within it a plethora of subtitles, because her job is literally endless.

Mothers are teachers, entertainers, chefs, housekeepers, nurses, coaches, referees, counselors, personal assistants, chauffeurs, event planners, stylists, finance managers, handy(wo)men, translators, dental hygienists, travel agents, personal trainers, lifeguards, psychic mind-readers, (mental, emotional, physical, and spiritual influencers), and sooooo much more to their children. And, moms perform the above (and all duties involved in *each* of these subtitles) *for FREE!*

Add an **income earned** to a mother's duties, and you get the kind of working mama *this* specific book targets. I feel it is impossible to sum up all things related to working mamas into one book (let alone one chapter!), so I've done my best to share as many mom-hacks on conscious parenting, career success, and true fulfillment into a few general topics that I'm passionate about. The following shaped me into the working mama I am today, and I hope you will gather many takeaways!

I believe that all mothers who are actively parenting their children are Working Mothers; and for most mothers, this continues to some degree or another until their very last breath.

MAMA'S GOTTA WORK . . . *FROM HOME.*

Full disclosure: I've never encountered more challenges than when I (try to) work from home. My current situation involves a toddler and an infant who have me on the clock 24 hours a day, 7 days a week, 365 days per year (actually, make that 366 . . . Yes, 2020, I'm counting!). It's nearly impossible to go more than ten consecutive minutes without interruption.

Being a stay-at-home-mama is a dream, as is working from home (for me); however, combining the two can be a lethal recipe for disaster. I operate an in-home business, and let me state here publicly: I've had far too many "business calls" with my baby on my hip and my toddler on my back . . . literally! Cue the eyeroll; so profesh.

What's even more challenging is solo-parenting, on top of all that. I'm not just talking about flying solo "some days" and "other nights." My husband is a contractor, and his work often takes him out of town for multiple days at a time. We take turns solo-parenting (thank gawd!), yet it still doesn't make it any easier when in the moment. I should also mention we live several hours away from our family and friends, so getting help from loved ones is just not an option, unfortunately.

Hiring help was the best decision I have made when it comes to working from home as a stay-at-home mama.

After hitting my **working-mama-max**, I made the conscious decision to hire someone to help me at home with my children for several hours a day, so I could *actually* get things done. As a parent, I do my best to be present and make conscious choices that serve my family and I in the highest regard—yet trying (unsuccessfully) to do it all on my own just wasn't working. Luckily I *did* have the choice of who I hired, so after screening through several reputable nanny websites online, I personally selected a great fit for my family.

As conscious parents, we must know our children's needs as well as our own. We need to keep the **big picture** in mind of what our ideal life looks and feels like, then work backwards and map out which steps we need to take to get there. I want my children to be happy, healthy, and whole—fully rounded as best as possible, and given infinite love, unwavering support, and plenty of safe space to discover and grow. So, after a thorough interview, then a meet-and-greet with the kids, I hired a wonderful nanny to come play with my babes a few days a week. This saved my sanity!

This also saved my career as a work-from-home mama, and it's the greatest investment I've made for my business! It took the extra pressure off my family, and allowed me to focus more on earning an income. The extra work I get done pays for my nanny's services and beyond, which is important to consider.

My hubby and I choose not to do childcare outside of the home at this time, so rather than me having to choose between growing my career, or having more time with my children, I choose to have *both!* I baked that cake, *and* ate the whole damn thing, too! My career has propelled exponentially since then, and I'm finally able to give my full attention to my work, *and* I can still be present with (and for) my children. Win, win!

I've come to the conclusion that *planning is crucial.* On Sundays I plan the week ahead, and create ways to buy myself "work time." We're minimalists and keep most toys in storage, because in our house: chaos breeds chaos, and chill breeds chill. Each morning I rotate "one toy out for every toy in" from storage, which keeps our kiddos occupied much longer than before. We borrow DVDs from our local library weekly, as that's the only screen-time they get, and one film a day keeps them entertained. We also have a small supply of educational dollar-store activities to use in desperate times. This makes for a few solid working hours throughout the day!

For me, true fulfillment is being able to pursue
my dreams while simultaneously being a
conscious, contributing, mindful mama!

Since becoming a mother, I've learned through trial and error what works well for me, and what doesn't. And though there are many ways to operate as a working mama, I cannot judge or condemn the decisions of others, nor would I wish the same in return. I believe we are all doing the best we can, and I understand that what gels for me may not gel with everyone—and vice-versa—and that's cool! *This* is what currently sparks *my* happy. You just do you, Mama!

MAMA'S GOTTA WORK . . . *AWAY FROM HOME.*

Throwback to my very first *back-to-work* experience after becoming a new mama. My firstborn was four months old, and I had been invited to perform at Canadian Music Week in Toronto. This was a big deal for someone in the music industry, and it was an opportunity I had been working toward for nearly a decade. I initially began performing recreationally as a young girl, and by my mid-twenties I was professionally pursuing an acting, singing, and writing career. Since then I've made a decent living in the entertainment business, and my career was blossoming until late in my first pregnancy.

The transition between *mom-life* and *work-life* seemed daunting at first. I was grateful and eager to be working more often again, as I had been missing my gigs dearly. I was also scared sh*tless everything would fall to pieces without me around. Plus, separation anxiety totally affects all of us, right?! Cue the rollercoaster ride!

Luckily I eased back into the game one gig at a time, and eventually worked my way up to being away from home for work for five consecutive days and nights per week. I'd work upwards of eighty hours a week on set, and be home as a *mombie* on the weekends. And guess what? Everything was okay! In fact, thanks to my incredible husband, everything was surprisingly better than ok. Praise be! What did I do, and how did *we* do it?

*First things first: we must be conscious of our thoughts and actions, deliberately choose the steps we are willing to take, and implement them into our lives accordingly. Then, most importantly, **we must let go of the rest**.*

I'm generally a very organized person. These days, my self-diagnosed OCD is more of an Organized Chaos Disorder because: kids. Since I knew I'd be working away from home one week at a time for several months (and useless at home on the weekends), I made a list *or: lists* (let's be honest, Krys!), to put on our chalkboard as guidelines for my husband to reference.

Now, he's not usually one to follow protocols per say, yet he did a great job of keeping our baby (and now babies) alive. And you know what? *That's what matters most!* I had no choice but to release the idea of everything being "just like I would do it." The simple act of me writing things down allowed me to get them out of my head, and I could walk away feeling confident I did my part. I let go of the nitty-gritty details, and gurl, it felt *SO* good!

We eventually have to put trust in someone other than ourselves to take care of our wee ones, and whether or not it's another parent, I promise the feelings of uncertainty subside. By trusting everything would be ok with my baby at home, I was able to better focus on my craft, which led to more job opportunities!

It wasn't easy for me that first day, despite how *perfect* our scenario may have seemed at a glance. My husband is a very free spirit, and could have been voted least-likely to become The World's Most Responsible Dad, before having kids. In fact, he's the guy that people jokingly said would be an untamed bachelor for life! Who knew he'd love taking turns staying home with the kids so much?!

This proves that by putting a little faith and trust in someone, it *will* nurture and grow their self-confidence, and miracles *can* happen! And the best part is: our children are happy, thriving, and so very well balanced between mama and dada time. Team baby-daddy-daycare, fo life!

Being able to select jobs that feel aligned with me, and having the freedom to mom-at-home (and mom-from-afar) is beyond fulfilling. My family and I get through each milestone together and apart, and I quickly realized that even if you miss something *BIG* (like your baby's very first steps, for example), the moment *you* witness them will still feel like the first time.

Thanks to modern day technology we're able to keep connected virtually through phone calls, picture messages, and video sharing. Talking openly with our kiddos and explaining to them why mama (or dada) will be away for work also goes a long way. Children understand more than most adults give them credit for, so this is something we've done in our family since day one, and it helps. Humans are resourceful—just embrace the changes as they come, and trust the process as it unfolds.

There will always be new learning curves: mentally, emotionally, physically, and even spiritually—Adaptability is the key that moves us forward.

MILK IT *'TIL YOU MAKE IT*, MAMA!

I've breast-pumped in some of the most questionable locations, on dozens of film sets throughout Ontario. On any day, you could find me behind the scenes searching for the perfect corner to set up my milking station. My scouting protocol was simple: if there are plugs, empty the jugs!

I quickly became a self-proclaimed pro-pumper, as I notoriously researched online for tips on how to increase my milk supply, and had my share of challenges in getting there. I was desperate to find ways to continue producing, while being gone for so long.

Those who work in the film industry will tell you the twelve to sixteen hour shifts on set are grueling. The lack of sleep between days, and next to no time for breaks on duty, is *no* joke! There is no set schedule when committed full time to a production, and it's a constant battle of mind and body to function normally, let alone produce milk.

On day one of my first day back, a colleague on set told me I "wouldn't last two weeks" when she saw me pumping during lunch, because "that's as far as she got before her milk dried up." Yikes! Up until that point, I hadn't been apart from my five-month-old for longer than six hours, and it was literally *just* the beginning of a three month shoot.

I chose to stick with my plan: pump as often as possible, keep my milk frozen on ice, bring it home to my baby, and nurse like a mofo on the weekends. I pre-pumped for several months prior to that (in between nursing my babe naturally), and built up a substantial supply. By then I had a great handle on what worked—specific foods to eat; teas to drink; essential oils to use; and tricks to perform to increase my milk production. I worked my tits off for it (pun intended!), and generally pumped thirty ounces daily. That's more than a twenty-sixer, for all my drankers out there ha-ha! I looked up my fair share of things online, and asked *all* around.

> *Researching everything I was experiencing for the first time helped make my overall experience as a working-mama much more pleasant.*

Mom-Hacks are plentiful in the virtual world, and if breastfeeding is something you're able to do, there are plenty of ways you can tell your tatas to "step the eff up!" I recommend getting familiar with terms like **Let-down**; **Foremilk** and **Hindmilk**; **When to Pump Between Feeds**; and

Dry-pumping too, if you haven't already done so. One of my favorite hacks is wearing an elastic bracelet that I switch back and forth from one wrist to the other, to help remember which side I ended with during the last feeding. You're welcome!

Producing milk is a supply and demand system: the more you milk, the more you make—which also means if you don't use it, you lose it. Experiment to learn what works for you. You just may end up swimming in liquid gold, to the point of leaking all over the floor in line at your local Starbucks, because you forgot to put breast-pads on. That may or may not have happened, to me. Ha!

No matter how many obstacles show up, and they will, it *is* possible to adapt when your *why* is clear. I consciously planned to feed my babies naturally for as long as I could, and that's exactly what I did. Consistency and perseverance are imperative. My babes never missed a feeding, and whether or not I was at home, they got mama's milk. This is a testament to my career success thus far, especially considering I spent four consecutive summers—either pregnant or pumping—while filming four seasons of the TV Series *Workin' Moms*. Legit, and fitting!

Both of my babies were equally young at five and six months old when I started back to work full time, and both of them breastfed for nearly a year and a half each. They are two very different babies, and there were many variables throughout the times. I believe my success is attributed to the power of having a positive mindset over most anything else, and I feel fulfilled and overjoyed as I reflect back upon it all in writing this. Big and small, we must always celebrate our wins, mamas!

YOU. ARE. *SUPERHUMAN!*

You are the only *you* that exists. To your children, you are a Queen; a Martyr; a Goddess. You have powers beyond this earthly realm, and your strength can withstand anything, even when you feel like crashing down in exhaustion. There is no-man like a wo-man, nor a greater force to be reckoned with!

No matter what you think you can or cannot do, you've always been and will always be a Super-Shero!

Be patient with yourself. Be patient with your partner, children, friends, family, colleagues, caregivers, and strangers too. Believe in yourself, and surrender to the process. You *will* find ways to navigate any unchartered waters. More is caught than taught, so learn from your personal experiences, and move forward with determination as only *you* are capable!

You *will* achieve success in your line of work, and you'll get a taste of failure too—that's okay. It's better to be a work in progress than to never try at all. You will adapt. You will grow into the status change to *mom in the workforce*. You will also maintain the most important role of being *mom at home*. You can be both (*you already are*), and if you don't know that yet, you will soon.

Stick together, mamas. True fulfillment can be found in endless ways—including being part of a collective. Join groups in your community, and socialize virtually, too. Ask questions. Talk about everything! Heck—reach out to me *anytime*—I will hold space for you. It takes a tribe, and no matter what age or stage you're at, I'd be honored to be part of your village. We are in this together, and it's time we join forces and blaze this Working Mama Force the eff-*UP!*

Conscious parenting while being a working mama can feel like a constant juggle between how we *aim* to parent, and how we *actually* parent. Being mindful of what we *wish* to do, and consistently applying that to what we *are* doing, helps keep us on track.

May you discover your deepest, purest, and truest feelings of fulfillment, dear mama. Just do your breast, and the rest will fall into place.

All my love and light to you,
Krysta Lee xox

Section two

Career Success:
Building a Mompire

FEATURING:

Pina Crispo
Amanda Drexler
Lisa Evans
Elizabeth Meekes
Michelle Emmick

Chapter Six

Just Keep Going from Here . . .

*"It's fuckin' exhausting trying to be
someone you are not."*

Pina Crispo

PINA CRISPO

www.ChicMamma.ca

ig: @chic_mamma | fb: @chicmamma | t: @chic_mamma

Pina Crispo

Not all mamas are created equal, and when it comes to Chic Mamma, Pina Crispo, you'll quickly learn just how unique she truly is!

What is Chic Mamma? It's the brand she solely founded in 2011 to help other mamas with their own unique children and parenting styles.

What makes her a unique mama? She is the ultimate radio chick host and producer of *The Parenting Show* on Global News Radio 640 Toronto (the ONLY parenting show on terrestrial radio in Canada). Pina is also a voice actor and voice coach. But wait! There's more! She also shares her passion and knowledge of radio and branding as a college professor at Humber College in Toronto where she teaches Media Branding and Creative Content Development in their Radio Broadcasting program.

Pina has always been one to want it all and do it all, and between the Chic Mamma brand and her radio and online personality, Pina truly embodies her brand.

She is an honest, authentic, true to life mama (with kids Samantha, Liliana, and Marcus) with style, humor, and all things in between. She tells it like it is and never holds back, which has been the foundation on which she has built her mama tribe.

Chic Mamma Pina Crispo . . . she's as real as it gets!

Just Keep Going from Here . . .

"We expect women to work like they don't have children, and raise children as if they don't work"

-Unknown

A few years back I came across this quote, it summed up my life at that moment, and who the fuck am I kidding, it still does! I don't know who wrote it, but man, I wish I did so I could give them a high five! But really, let's think about that for a minute, it's bang on don't you think? Talk about having your cake and eating it too!

Allow me introduce myself, my name is Pina, and I wasn't always a mom. To be honest, I've spent the majority of my life *not* being one, and that only changed nine years ago at the age of thirty-one. At the time I was the head of the marketing and promotions department for one of the top alternative rock radio stations in Canada. Radio was my first love, and all I've ever known career wise since I was sixteen. I lived and breathed radio twenty-four, seven there was no turning it off. It was who I was, it ran through my veins, and it was what was going on inside my head.

Let's rewind to 2011, I was pregnant with my first child, Samantha. I remember the nine-month mark approaching; maternity leave was around the corner. I was excited and scared all at once. Excited because I was going to have a baby, and scared because I didn't know WTF to do or expect. I wondered if I would be a good mom, if I was even cut out for it, and let's not forget the work side of things and what a year off on mat-leave would mean for me. This was just some of the shit that occupied my overthinking brain. It was all the what if's, and different scenarios I would play out over and over again.

Ready or not, this baby was coming, and there was no turning back.

On June 24, 2011, I gave birth to Samantha and let me tell you, she was beyond perfect. I remember taking her home and being so in love with her. For the first time in what seemed like forever, I didn't have anything to focus on, but her. And while I was feeling all these amazing things with my newborn in my arms, I also felt something else, something I couldn't explain. It was a sense of not belonging, loneliness, and feeling lost; like I didn't know who I was anymore. Sitting at the kitchen table with my husband while Samantha was sleeping, I just broke down crying. Nick looked at me and asked me what was wrong, but I just remember saying "I don't know." It was weird, we left the house as two people, but we came back three, and my whole life was suddenly different. I went from working twenty-four, seven in an industry that I loved, being surrounded by people all the time, and hitting up concerts a few nights a week to being at home, alone, with a baby—and no human interaction besides my husband, parents, and occasionally my sisters. I felt guilty for feeling this way. I shouldn't feel guilty, I have a beautiful and healthy baby girl, a roof over my head, food on the table, and everything was more than good—it was great!

It was at that point that the depression started to creep in, and I realized something needed to be done. I am not one to sit down, do nothing, and be cool with it. I live a fast-paced life, and need to work. If you haven't figured it out yet I'm what people call a "work alcoholic." I was grieving human interaction, and needed to keep busy. I knew shit-all about being a mom, and thought to myself: *If I'm feeling like this, I wonder how many others are feeling the same way?*

I needed a solution, and when I couldn't find it,
I decided to create it myself.

It was then that my Chic Mamma's Facebook group was born. It was a group for myself and some close friends who were new moms and losing their minds much like I was. It was a place to come together, share stories, exchange notes, get advice, and feel somewhat *normal* because no matter how alone you feel as a new mom, you realize that there are other people out there experiencing the same thing you are, or a version of it at least. We would laugh, cry, and share each other's company during those lonely and exhausting 3:00 a.m. feedings. Quickly that group grew, and with moms from all over the world. I started to feel a little bit better, I had my group that I moderated and was admin of, which gave me a purpose and kept me a little busy—but it wasn't enough. So in addition to the blog I was writing for the radio station (which focused on the alt rock lifestyle), I decided to create my own blog, focused on this new life of motherhood: ChicMamma.ca! I was writing, my little community was growing, all while being a mom and having fun with Samantha. I even partnered up with the baby company Munchkin Canada and started to write weekly Munchkin Mondays reviews. I had a groove going. It wasn't radio, but I was feeling good and that lasted for a bit—until the week before returning to work.

I'll never forget that moment when my phone rang, it was my boss calling to tell me that there was no job for me to return to. Cue the depression, once again. Like what the fuck?! I have worked my whole life, and now here I am with a kid in my arms and jobless. My dream job, the job I loved so much, gone just like that. I was thirty-two years old, and had been in radio for exactly half of my life—it was ripped away from me. I went to school for radio broadcasting, not marketing, not promotions, or even public relations. Radio . . . I went to school for RADIO! I remember thinking to myself *what the fuck am I gonna do now?* I have a diploma and there were no radio jobs in the Toronto market especially for a pregnant woman.

Yup, that's right, I was pregnant with kiddo number two. I was a mess, and although I loved Samantha and baby on the way, I was miserable. I just wanted to work and do the things I loved, but instead I was a stay-at-home mom, resenting my husband for being able to escape to work, while I with a kid on the boob, and feeling like ass due to pregnancy (yes I'm one of them, I hated being pregnant). Oh, and let's not forget the part where I was trying my best to fit the *perfect mom mold,* and let me tell you, I'm no June Cleaver. I was a shit show, I won't lie, but I had to go on, so I continued to run my Facebook group and blog. It was at that point I remember thinking to myself: *maybe this social media stuff I'm doing has legs; maybe I can take my skills and work experience in marketing, promotions, public relations, and social media, and turn this into a sustainable business—and work for myself*, so that's what I did.

I knew that if I wanted to give this a shot, now was the time.

I started to work on all things Chic Mamma, beginning with updating my website with a team overseas that was twelve hours ahead of us, so while I was up breastfeeding, I would email them changes, approvals, etc. I decided it was time to trademark Chic Mamma, and I began to explore ways to monetize because now I needed to make money if I wanted this to work. I was working around the clock, and it felt great to be doing my own thing; not having to answer to anyone and having the ability to say yes or no when needed. Was it easy? Fuck no! I was busting my ass, working crazy hours, still trying to be the perfect mom. Did I mention that I was pregnant and miserable as fuck? 'Cuz I was!

Months passed, and before I knew it, it was May 14, 2013, and my second daughter Liliana was born. I'll never forget lying in my hospital bed and getting a call from the program director for a new radio station launching in Toronto; there was a promotions director position available. I was so thrilled to be considered but the problem was that they needed someone to start in September—only four months away and I was torn! Do I cut my maternity leave short and go back? An industry that I loved and missed dearly, but also an industry that had kicked me to the curb nearly one year before? Do I go for it and forfeit my maternity leave, knowing there's no getting it back if things don't work out, and do I really want to miss out on Lily's first year because of a job? I love radio, and wanted this gig so bad, but I loved my girls more. I let them know that unfortunately the timing was not ideal and prayed that I did the right thing.

So here I was, juggling life with a newborn and toddler, while working for myself. I had all things Chic Mamma going, as well as my voice acting (my side hustle since graduating college). There was no kicking back and chilling out, 'cuz mamas gotta work right?! I kept grinding away because no work means no money. Everything in my company continued to grow, but doing it all with two kids wasn't easy. So, what do I do when things are crazy? I make them crazier and take on more. Lily was one when I was offered a part time position at Humber College to be the professor for their new media branding class for the second year radio broadcasting students. It was radio mixed with social media, and a foot back into the radio world; all while allowing me to be with the girls, work on Chic Mamma, and getting me out of the house. It was rewarding to be back and walk down the familiar hallways of Humber and teach in the same classes I was taught in. It felt amazing, and it still does. Eventually, from teaching; media branding and (I was also given) the creative content development class, which had me at the school once a week for the full school year; my plate was full, but what choice do you have when you work for yourself—you don't! Bring it on!

*One way or another, you make it all work—
even with two kids under three, and another
on the way.*

Yup, baby number three was on the way, and there was no slowing down anytime soon. It was a challenging time because on top of the kids and work, I was also dealing with my dad who had been battling cancer for a few years. No one ever prepared me on how to deal with shit when a loved one is sick. It's scary and you feel helpless, complete-ly and utterly helpless. July 2015 rolled around and my dad was in the hospital, and I was going back and forth, back and forth, with both girls by my side. I remember seeing my dad's health steadily decline, and trying to hold my fuckin' shit together for the sake of my dad, mom, and my kids—even though I was dying inside because as much as I hated to admit it, I was losing my dad. My dad made it back home, but within a matter of weeks he passed, and nothing in life could have prepared me for that moment. On July 25, 2015, I watched my dad take his last breath and die; it was the worst, most horrible thing I have ever experienced. It's gut-wrenching, and it leaves you with a broken heart that you soon realize is beyond repair. I was also six months pregnant with Marcus, a grandchild that he would never meet.

Three months later and still mourning the loss of my dad, Marcus was born! It was October 15, 2015, and I was now a mom of three; Sa-mantha (four), Liliana (two), and Marcus. I remember everyone telling me that going from two kids to three is a breeze; they said, "you barely even notice a difference," "it would be fun," they said a lot of things—and you wanna know what? It was fuckin' killer, they conveniently left that part out haha. A big thing about being an entrepreneur, there is no maternity leave—you gotta work, and your income is all based on how hard you work. I was up pretty much twenty-four, seven between the kids, Marcus feedings all-night, and work. There was no time for sleep if I wanted to get it all done, this was a one-woman-show, no employ-ees or help, 'cuz it wasn't in the budget, which means no passing work onto someone else, or even shutting things down for a bit. Many people don't see this side of things, they just think it's awesome that you have a successful business. There was hard work, hustling, and grinding away, it wasn't a walk in the park, and something still didn't feel right. As the kids got older, there was a shift inside of me—and one day it just hit me like a ton of bricks, I wasn't happy!

For years I was trying to fit in and be the perfect mom, but I was missing the person I was; the person I hid away because I thought that I had to act a certain way since I was now a mom. It's fuckin' exhaust-ing trying to be someone you are not. I was done, and decided it was time for the return of the real Pina. What once scared me, I didn't care about anymore; I had zero fucks to give. I was done with giving a shit about what people had to say about me or even think of me. That's how I was before kids, and I was ready to welcome it back with open arms. I was ready to once again be my truly unapologetic self. I knew this would maybe mean a dip in my numbers on my site and readers on my blog, and in my audience on social media, but I was ready for it. The funny thing was that when I came out guns-blazing, nothing happened! I didn't get any nasty emails or DMs, and in fact, I was getting a positive response.

People liked it because I was saying and doing things that they only ever thought about, but never acted on, and it was refreshing for them to see.

It was as if a weight was lifted off my shoulders. I was back, and I was once again doing things for myself and putting myself first, including my happiness. For the longest time I thought I was *just* a mom, but the truth is that we are never *just* moms, we are more! We are individuals, and when we are happy and take care of ourselves, we can then be better to the people around us—and that includes our children. It made me realize that this whole time what I was missing from my life was myself, a piece of me had died and it felt so good to be resurrected. I quickly noticed a change and people were engaging more, and more work opportunities came my way.

It all started with a call I got from Sandra Carusi, she said "P, I have an idea!" Right then I knew it was gonna be something crazy, but doable, because it was coming from Sandra. Sandra and I have a history in radio together—she was in sales while I was in marketing and promotions. Sandra was a go-getter and made shit happen no matter how crazy or big her ideas were. Now, although I had been gone for six years from the radio station, and Sandra was on medical leave for cancer treatment, that didn't stop her from coming up with ideas and dreams. Much like me, Sandra needed to keep busy—the more work the better—and so although she was off work, she created a few passion projects which were radio shows. She started by hosting and producing the comedy, *Inside Jokes*, on AM640, then producing *The Dating and Relationship Show*, and finally (and this is where I came in), she had an idea for another show: *The Parenting Show*. She asked me to host. My own radio show? *The Parenting Show* with Pina Crispo of ChicMamma. ca sounded pretty sweet, I won't lie. Sandra told me she wanted a real mom to host the show, a mom who tells it like it is, and doesn't sugar coat shit. She said "P, I want to bring Chic Mamma and your blog to life on radio, let's do it," and so we did.

February 26, 2017, and we were on the air. *The Parenting Show* on Global News Radio 640 Toronto, which happens to be the only parenting show on terrestrial radio in Canada. It was a dream come true, all because of Sandra. Things were all falling into place, I was doing my thing, and it felt great. Finally I was comfortable with who I was as a person again, and as a mom. ChicMamma.ca was doing well, Humber College was great, and now the radio show. We were on a roll and having a blast—until August 13, 2018, when Sandra lost her battle with cancer, leaving behind her two boys that she loved and adored, Patrick and Luke, as well as her three radio shows.

Never in a million years did I think life was going to pan out like this for me. I always thought that I would continue working full time in corporate radio. Never did I think my career would be in social media creating content, teaching in the radio broadcasting program, doing voice acting, and of course hosting and producing *The Parenting Show*—alongside my new co-host who is one of the most amazing and talented females in broadcasting, Jennifer Valentyne. The past nine years of being a mom has flipped my world upside down and right side up again.

The curve balls will keep on coming, I know that, but fuck, we're moms, and we'll hit each and every one of them outta the park, even if you're down a strike or two.

Chapter Seven

Some Moms Run a Tight Ship, I Run a Tight Shipwreck

"It's been fifteen years, I haven't won the mother of the year award yet! My kids are still alive; that's worth a participation ribbon, isn't it?"

Amanda Drexler

AMANDA DREXLER

www.drexlertravel.com
ig: @drexlertravel | fb: @drexlertravel

Amanda Drexler

Amanda is an award-winning luxury family travel specialist. She lives in the small town of Fergus, Ontario with her two teens and her husband of almost twenty years. She is active in her community and enjoys helping not-for-profits both locally and globally. While she is a proud Canadian, she loathes the winter months. It never takes too much convincing to get her on a plane to explore new tropical destinations, try a great cocktail . . . or three, and indulge in the local cuisine. She believes nothing in life makes you richer than travel, so invest in memories and not things.

Some Moms Run a Tight Ship, I Run a Tight Shipwreck

This past Christmas my daughter gave me a gift. It was a plaque that said, "I considered being a stay-at-home mom, but then I realized the kids would be there." I laughed, we all laughed. This gift could have offended or hurt me, but it did not; it was the truth!

I remember being in college and hearing some girls in my program tell one of our professors they aspired to be stay-at-home moms. I remember thinking how sad that was. Did they not have any other dreams or goals? Now, don't go getting your panties in a knot if you're a stay-at-home mom reading this.

The thought of being a stay at home mom just didn't fulfill me. I knew I wanted kids one day, but I had dreams of having my own business.

My first business was a full-service salon. Three years later I became pregnant. As my first trimester passed, I worried I wouldn't get to enjoy my first crack at motherhood while running a business, so I listed the business for sale. Two days before our son was born, the sale of my salon went through. I was officially a stay-at-home mom. Nine months down the road I was itching to get back to work and to feel like I had something of my own again. Is it bad that the first day I dropped our son off at daycare I didn't cry? I was so excited for pure adult time again!

Mamas listen closely: you may feel like scum of the earth dropping your kiddo off for the first day of daycare, especially if it doesn't go well, but here's the thing, my kids still reminisce about their days at daycare, chicken pox parties, lice parties . . . oh right, I'm supposed to bring light to this daycare thing. Ok, seriously it's one of the best things you can do for your kids! They learn to be social, gain some independence, and they meet friends. My son still has his bestie from daycare fourteen years later, I gained another son, and a new drinking buddy: his mom! Win, win!

There should be no guilt in wanting to be a mom, a wife, and have a successful career. I think we just need to learn to let go of perfection and realize living a perfectly imperfect life is ok.

Being a working mom is in my blood: my mom was a nurse who retired to work full-time in our family business. Her mom worked through motherhood into her retirement years. We are women who are not afraid of hard work, and I am grateful for the work ethic they have instilled in me, and the lessons I learned from them.

My mom likes to remind me often of how lucky I am to have the husband I do, and that my dad or other men from that generation wouldn't do half the things he does. Case in point, I observed early on and knew that I wanted a marriage that would be more 50-50, than 80-20. I should remind my mom how lucky dad is to have her!

This brings me to another point of WHY I am proud to be a working mom and have my career. Our kids have grown up watching their mom and dad work together. There is no household task they haven't seen either of us do. I may have been fired from cutting the grass, but that's another story, and it might have been intentional on my part . . . The point is, they have not grown up with the mentality of "that's a man's job," or "that's a woman's job."

My second point is I want my daughter to know (through my actions) that she can have big dreams and goals, and that having kids doesn't mean her life stops. Having a husband that contributes equally to our family also shows her what a healthy marriage can look like. Oh, baby girl! Daddy has set the bar high! Equally important, I want our son to grow up knowing the importance of having a spouse that will encourage him to live his best life, while he reciprocates this for her.

We all know having a relationship that is fifty-fifty is key, but this really is just a figure of speech. Let's be real! Some moms run a tight ship, I run a tight shipwreck. Some weeks I work thirty hours, some weeks I work sixty hours. Our kids are both in rep sports and between my husband and I, we are present at ninety-five percent of their activities. There are days I am working as I sit on the sidelines, and days I am out of the country. Life happens and sometimes you have to sacrifice to achieve the big goals you have set for you and your family, which means you or your spouse may do more of the heavy lifting some weeks than the other. *No* guilt in that, mamas.

In the summer of 2015 I had surgery, which put a halt on my regular activities resulting in having a lot more time to think. This was both a blessing and a curse. It was a blessing because it gave me the time to think about the last few years and all the lessons I learned, as well as all of the professional development I had done. This gave me the strength to get through the next few months and the strength to ask for help when I needed to battle some demons. I was in my fourth year with a network marketing company; I worked alongside family and friends and met so many other amazing human beings. I had reached a level in my business many dreamed of reaching, and yet part of me just wasn't happy. I didn't know if I had it in me or wanted to go to the next level of my business. I felt like a fraud. So, I made a list of the pros and the cons. In the end, the pros were not enough to keep me in the game. This is where the curse of having too much time to think came in. All the thoughts of who I would let down came rushing in. Was I teaching my kids it was ok to quit? What about all those times I said I was in this for *life*? It was a downward spiral. The hardest part was being told I needed to keep my exit on the down low. My team was family, family is who we go to in hard times and now I felt like I couldn't talk to them.

I realized if I wasn't taking care of number one I couldn't take care of anyone effectively. I had to dig deep and figure out what my love language was.[1] I had to realize changing my path was not quitting. I was following my heart and teaching my kids to follow their heart and do what makes them happy. Discovering what made me tick didn't take long. Travel has always been an immense love of mine, so when I was presented with the opportunity to work from home as an independent travel agent, I was intrigued—to say the least. I jumped in with both feet!

If I've shown my kids anything, it is not to be afraid to take a risk; and that often when something scares you shitless, and excites you all at once, it is likely something you should pursue.

My business as a travel agent offers many travel opportunities, some purely for fun and other times for work. I know, I know, it's a "tough gig," but someone has to do it. I hear your comments: "Oh it must be nice." "Don't you feel bad leaving your family?" "Do you ever work?" It used to bother me, now it's just like hearing Charlie Brown say, "wah, wah,

---

1   Gary Chapman, "The 5 Love Languages," Moody Bible Institute (website), last modified June 6, 2007, https://www.5lovelanguages.com/book/the-5-love-languages/.

wah, wah, wah." Here's the thing, some people are joking with their comments and some are not. It's not my job to figure out why they are not happy with their lives. The reality is the only person who can change your life is *you*. So, if you're not happy in your career, in your relationships, with your health or whatever it may be; what are *you* going to do to make a change?

My life is far from perfect! But as I tell my kids, I don't ask them to strive for perfection; I ask them to wholeheartedly give it all they've got. There is no such thing as failures, only lessons; and I have had my share of lessons!

I've got two teenagers in my house now . . . believe me I am learning a lot! Mostly from my fifteen-year-old because he knows *everything*. I thought the terrible twos were hard . . . *ha*! I remember my cousin saying to me one day (prior to her having kids), "I don't remember you drinking this much when we were younger." I laughed and said, "just wait until you have kids." She understands now.

Did you know there are fifteen national booze days you should be celebrating?! Starting with number one, February 22, National Margarita Day. Number ten, July 10, is National Pina Colada Day. This may be one of my favorites. My kids know I like them so much that on one family holiday my daughter may have yelled out, "Mom, isn't it Pina Colada time?" and it may have only been 10:00 a.m. I sat up looking around, like *where is her mother?* When you get to number twelve it gets a little risky, July 12 is National Tequila Day. This is where I need to bow out as I am allergic. True story: it makes my clothes fall off! I told you, not going for perfection, right?

We all have our days. I have days I feel so strong I could conquer the world and then I have days I want to throw in the towel. Surrounding myself with women who lift and encourage me has been a huge reason why I can move past those challenging days. Thank you to those who are a listening ear, those who make me laugh until we cry or pee a little (keeping it real), and to those who can call me out on my shit when I need it.

We need to teach our daughters to be women who build each other up, rather than tear each other apart.

I haven't always made the best choices in those I surrounded myself with, however after many lessons you learn to listen to your gut and pay close attention to how someone makes you feel. It took me a long forty years to dig deep and be okay with who I am, to stop wanting to be a people-pleaser, to understand that there will be those who love me and those who won't. Mamas, just be you! It's so much harder trying to be the person others want you to be.

Taking care of number one also means learning to say *no*. This was a very challenging thing for me. People-pleasers want to help everyone and often experience major FOMO (Fear Of Missing Out). I had my hand in so many activities at one point. This created a lack of focus, and a lack of fulfillment because I was burning the candle at both ends. I had to become laser focused, and prior to committing to anything, ask myself *will this activity bring me closer to my goals and dreams?* I'm not just talking about business goals and dreams. I am talking about personal goals too. Some people thrive on jam-packed schedules and don't like quiet time. I am not that mama! Maybe this is an over forty thing . . . but I love having a Friday or Saturday night with *nothing* on the calendar! I am perfectly okay with leaving one night a week with absolutely nothing scheduled. These are the nights we often find time for spontaneous date nights or maybe games with the kids. By the way, to fifteen-year-olds, this is a form of torture. Having a free night sometimes means saying no to family or friend events too. When it comes to your sanity, sometimes something's gotta give.

Remember to make time for each other as a family, and as a couple.

Our careers are a huge part of our lives and what makes us tick, but do you work to live or live to work? I work to live! Living is seeing my kids experience a new country for the first time, connecting with another child who speaks another language with a simple smile, the four of us walking on a beach with no devices in hand and connecting as a family, or watching the two kids fight over who gets the window seat on the plane while my husband and I sit five rows ahead in the seats we purposely booked away from them. Mamas please don't forget your family started as two. My husband and I do all we can to get away at least one week a year as a couple. I realize an entire week might not work for every couple, but it's amazing what even a long weekend can do. The kids will survive, your businesses or careers will survive your time away, and what you might find most shocking: your relationships and your careers will thrive because you've filled your cup and taken care of number one.

Chapter Eight

Choosing the Mom and Businesswoman I Want to Be

"To be successful at running my business and being a mom, I needed to accept that every decision I make about where I put my energy and time is a choice and that I am in charge of that choice."

Lisa Evans

LISA EVANS

https://thiscaffeinatedmama.com | www.chickadeefamilycafe.com
ig: @thismamarunsoncoffee

Lisa Evans

Lisa Evans began her career as a freelance writer for magazines and newspapers across Canada and is now the owner of Chickadee Family Café, the first ever play café in Burlington, Ontario. Lisa created this family friendly space to help mamas like her, who were struggling to make new connections in their community. Lisa is mama to Nathan and Abigail, wife to Chris, and resides in Burlington, Ontario.

Choosing the Mom and Businesswoman I Want to Be

January 5, 2015, I was in a hospital bed at St. Joseph's in Toronto. Around my twelfth hour of labour, my phone dinged and I instinctively checked it. It was an email from one of my editors asking if I had time to take on an assignment. "I'm actually in labour right now," I replied. "I'm taking the next three weeks off to focus on the baby, but if you have any assignments after that, I'd be happy to take it on."

I was a freelancer, writing articles for magazines and newspapers across North America. I spent most of my days on the phone conducting interviews with experts; from medical doctors to business owners, professors and book authors. In the evenings, and in between interviews, I would write the articles. I knew I'd have to scale back my workload when my baby was born and I knew my post-baby workdays would look different, but had no idea how different they would be.

One afternoon when my son was nearly a month old, I had a phone interview with a psychologist for an article about why emotionally intelligent people make more money. I had hoped my son would nap during the call, but when the scheduled time rolled around he was still wide awake. There I was nursing him while leaning into the speaker phone, the voice recorder beside it because I couldn't type notes. I was trying my best to ask intelligent questions to this professor while my shirt was half off, my raw nipples exposed and aching, and I just hoped my baby would fall asleep on the boob and not cry out. Scheduling phone interviews with a baby, I learned, was like playing a game of roulette.

> *I realized then I'd have to make a choice about my life as a new mom. I could quit my work and focus one-hundred percent of my attention on raising my babe, or I could find help and make a go of the working mom life.*

THE CHOICE TO BE A WORKING MOM

Growing up, my mom was a stay-at-home mom. She returned to the workforce when I was around ten years old landing the perfect job as a school receptionist, giving her summers and holidays off to spend with my sister and I. Work was always a fourth thought to her; coming after myself, my sister, and my dad. I don't remember my mom ever talking about career ambitions. She loved her job and often spoke of the camaraderie at the workplace, but never spoke about wanting more for her career. My vision of motherhood was this incredibly patient woman who devoted herself to raising her kids, who planned crafts every day, read books, decorated cupcakes, played board games, always had time for her kids, and genuinely enjoyed spending time in *mom mode* with them. I knew I had a rockstar mom, and part of me wanted to be just like her, but I also knew deep down I'd feel unfulfilled if I stopped working altogether.

I felt a great sense of purpose in my work. I loved that my job gave me the opportunity to learn something new every single day; not to mention I got to interview some incredible people, including some big name local celebrities. I had interviewed *CBC Dragons* Brett Wilson and Manjit Minhas, *HGTV* star builder Bryan Baeumler, and Canadian money maven Gail Vaz-Oxlade.

I'd always said I felt fulfilled by my work, but as a new mom, suddenly saying that I loved my job seemed to translate to saying that I wasn't completely fulfilled being a mom. I had wanted to be a mom for so long. I had wanted to be just like *my* mom and now that I had the baby I'd dreamed of for years right there in my arms, I felt guilty saying that I wanted more in my life. I thought there was something wrong with me as a new mom that I wasn't content simply being with my baby, attending mommy and me classes, and experimenting with homemade baby purees. This urge to work was always sitting there on the surface, nagging at me, saying "you should be doing more." I didn't just *want* to work. I *needed* to work.

The more I thought about not being the mom I had, the more guilty I felt. I finally realized I needed to create my own definition of a "good mom". I had a great mom. But that didn't mean that I had to have her life in order to be a great mom too.

I decided that I wanted to be the mom who raised her son to know that his mama has dreams, passions, ambitions, and goals that existed before and apart from him. I would be the mom that baked him the Paw Patrol cake he wanted for his birthday, but also as the mom whose name appeared in print in major publications.

Being a working mother, though, would require some help, unless I wanted to keep doing interviews with my shirt half off.

I decided to dedicate two mornings a week to my work, and found a wonderful nanny to come to my house twice a week for two hours at a time, to watch over my month-old son while I went into my home office and made phone calls. This time blocking allowed me to fulfill that urge to work and also allowed me to enjoy the time that I wasn't working; the time that I was being mama. This routine worked great for seven months until the day our world was shaken.

WHEN WORKING MAMA IS NO LONGER A CHOICE

When my son was eight months old, my husband was diagnosed with Osteosarcoma, bone cancer. The next ten months were filled with aggressive in-hospital chemotherapy, surgery, and months of recovery.

Holy shit! We had just purchased a house in Burlington, Ontario. Chris' biopsy was scheduled the day before we were to move into our new family home. I received a phone call around two in the afternoon that day saying he wasn't leaving the hospital. I felt my entire life had just flipped upside down. I was the girl who always had a plan. I had envisioned myself spending my days between writing in my home office and attending mommy and me music classes with my son. Now I was staring at a blank canvas and I had no idea what I was going to paint on it. My son and I moved into our family home by ourselves; a home that was over an hour-and-a-half away from the Toronto hospital where Chris was being treated. I spent many nights alone on the couch worrying about the kind of life we were going to have.

We had a $400,000 mortgage and the person responsible for paying seventy percent of our living expenses would now receive only sixty percent of his salary for at least the next year. If I stayed working two mornings a week, we weren't sure we'd be able to keep the house we'd just purchased; the house we'd imagined raising and growing our family in.

I found a home daycare around the corner and kicked into full-time freelancing gear, then six months later landed a full-time nine to five marketing job. It wasn't the life I'd envisioned, but I felt I was doing what I had to do and I convinced myself I could find the same fulfilment I had in my entrepreneurial freelance life within the corporate world; the one that came with a biweekly paycheck, benefits and paid time off.

Flash forward a couple of years. Chris was recovered and back at his job. I had been sitting behind a desk, pumping out marketing campaigns. I loved my job for the same reasons my mom probably loved hers. The camaraderie, the holiday parties, the steady paycheck. But there was something missing. When I was a freelance writer, I felt that I was making an impact in our community by telling people's stories, spreading awareness and education.

Having a paycheck and *a job*, it seemed, wasn't enough for me. I needed to be doing something that I cared about and that ultimately my son would be proud of. Well, I guess he'd be proud to have parents with a house that's paid off and money in their RRSPs, but I felt my purpose behind the desk was simply to make someone else rich.

It wasn't just that I was feeling mom guilt about being a working mother, I was feeling out of alignment with myself.

THE BIRTH OF A NEW CAREER

When my son was a toddler, I'd trek him out to a café on weekends to treat myself to a Sunday latte. The coffee dates nearly always ended with him flinging his toys on the ground and my latte barely having a sip out of it before we had to leave; often after receiving glares from other café patrons who clearly didn't enjoy the raging tantrum of a two-year-old who now didn't want the blueberry muffin he'd demanded mere seconds before.

One day instead of the coffee shop jaunt, I took him to an indoor playground. After chasing him around for an hour, getting a bump on the head from going down the child-size slide, anxiously wiping him down 'cause ick, germs, and looking around at all the parents who seemed to be exhausted and bored . . . I had a thought: wouldn't it be lovely if there was a place that offered the coffee I wished I had in my hand at that moment paired with a safe place for kids to play? At the time I was seeing numerous mom groups pop up online, but there didn't seem to be many places for those moms to meet up in person and chat.

Can you smell opportunity? I could.

I knew I'd found my purpose: to create a family-oriented space that brought the parenting village together. I started the process of opening a family-friendly café that would provide the coffee shop experience for adults while also providing a fun space for kids to play, explore, and interact with their peers. How amazing would it be, I thought, to create this space for families in our community and in the process teach my son there is more than one path to a career, and if you don't find the career that fulfills you in the marketplace, you can create your own.

I opened Chickadee Family Café in March 2019 and became a full-time mompreneur!

THE CHALLENGES OF MOMPRENEUR LIFE

As a mompreneur, I was constantly pulled to be a mom and a business owner simultaneously. When I was being praised by our customers for bringing this much-needed space to our community, my home life was now in chaos. My husband was exhausted after being pulled into a full-time daddy role on top of his full-time work role. I was struggling to stay on top of everything required to run the business. I was the barista, the accountant, the marketer, the cleaner. Oh and yes, mama and wife too. I was trying to do everything and I was failing. I built a business that was all about serving young families and yet my own family was falling apart. How could I have got this all wrong?

It wasn't until I realized that every decision about where I put my time and effort was actually my choice that I saw things clearly.

*To be successful at running my business and being a mom, I needed to accept that every decision I make about where I put my energy and time is a **choice** and that **I am in charge of that choice**.*

Unlike my corporate days, as an entrepreneur, no one was telling me how to do any of the jobs on my plate. No one was dictating my operating hours. No one was telling me I had to put on ten events a month. No one was telling me I couldn't hire an accountant to take some load off of me. Similarly, no one was telling me I had to be the mom who volunteered to run the bake sale at school. No one was telling me I had to hand-make my son's Halloween costume instead of buying one at Costco. In order to pull off this mompreneur life, I needed to adjust my expectations of motherhood and my expectations of me as a business owner.

The first major change I made was in my business' operating hours. When I opened my business, I set my hours from 8:00 a.m. to 6:00 p.m. Stay open as long as possible to get as much business as possible, I thought. What this meant in reality though is that I left home at seven in the morning and didn't get home until seven at night. Most days my son would come to the café after school and spend the last hour or so with me at work, but getting home late meant that we ate dinner at eight and my son was having a hard time winding down, often not going to bed until ten! Our home life was chaotic, and we were missing out on quality time together.

When I thought about my days, I realized those last two hours were quiet at the café with only a few guests. So I changed my hours, 9:00 a.m to 4:00 p.m. I would get to pick my son up from school every day, take him to swimming lessons and to baseball games in the evenings, and have dinner as a family.

The decision to close at 4:00 p.m. wasn't easy, and I received a few messages along the lines of "your café is only good for stay-at-home moms," even though I was open on weekends too. But there weren't enough evening customers to justify paying a staff person to cover those hours, and I needed to choose my family over the few extra dollars I could make at the close of the day.

*I needed to set boundaries and create blocks of **work time** and **mom time**.*

This time blocking felt like my earlier freelance days. That separation of *work life* and *mom life* had helped to ease the guilt of the time I spent working and allowed me to enjoy both these times separately from the other, and fully.

There are times when I have to choose between work and family, in particular on weekends when we host birthday parties or participate in festivals to market the business. Family doesn't always win, but when I choose work, I know I'm doing it consciously. I may choose the birthday party over family time because I know that birthday parties are an important source of revenue for the business. The festivals are important to raise awareness of the business and I try to choose ones that my son can come and participate in so we can still sneak in that mommy-son time.

My business may not become a billion-dollar empire. It may simply be the local family-run shop that fulfilled a need in our small community of Burlington, Ontario. I don't think I've fully developed myself as a business woman yet, but I do have a much clearer picture of the mom I am and want to be. I want to teach my children that there is more than one path to a fulfilling life and career. I want my children to see that their mom (and by extension, all women) can be both mom *and* CEO. I want my children to see their mom as a woman who has goals and ambitions that exist separate from them, but not at the expense of them. While I felt a tremendous amount of guilt about wanting to be a working mama in my early mom days, I now believe that being a working mom is the best gift I can give to my children. If I have taught them any of these lessons, I'll be proud of the mom I've become.

Chapter Nine

The Fire in my Soul

"I needed myself outside of the me that is mom."

Elizabeth Meekes

ELIZABETH MEEKES

www.elizabethmeekes.com
ig: @lizmeekes | fb: @lizmeekes

Elizabeth Meekes

Elizabeth Meekes is a coach, holistic practitioner, numerologist, writer, podcaster, speaker, entrepreneur, and eternal student of the Universe. She completed a Bachelor of Arts at Wilfrid Laurier University where she found her passion in radio and was recognized for her work with Radio Laurier.

As a holistic practitioner, Elizabeth is passionate about health and wellness. When it felt as if her love of learning was missing from her life and business, this inner calling pushed her to become a certified life coach through the Centre for Applied Neuroscience. Elizabeth is committed to consistent growth and learning and believes that the greatest investment we can make is in ourselves. Following that commitment, she continues to learn from her own mentors/coaches, who have included Gabby Bernstein, Anne Beauvais, and Harriette Hale.

Elizabeth is passion, determination, strength, and love. She is a spiritual gangster: deeply connected to the power of the universe. Her mission is to create massive change in this world through being raw and true in her power, standing back up every time she falls, and empowering you to do the same. She shares this incredible life with her partner Steve and their two boys, Rowan and Arion.

The Fire in my Soul

I had my first baby when I was twenty-two. The following spring I learned I was pregnant with my second. Two babies fifteen months apart at twenty-three . . . cool.

The babies definitely surprised me. There wasn't a whole lot of time to figure out what I wanted to do with my life before them, and once they came, it was as if that was all I knew. Mothering felt natural. Ironic, really. I never wanted children, and now here I was mommying with the best of them. I settled in and got comfortable. At least until I realized how trapped I felt inside my world.

I was screaming inside.

I *should* want to stay home with my babies right? I *should* be thrilled, so many women would just dream of being home with their children. These were only stories I was telling myself. *Should* is a dirty word, attaching us to unrealistic expectations. I felt guilt for wanting to work and create, when I had the option to stay home. But, as much as I adore my kids, that wasn't what I wanted.

I needed myself outside of the me that is mom.

It was like I had this pull, this inner knowing that I could be a great mom and also so many other things. It wasn't about staying home, or going to work. It was about finding and creating space for me, and recognizing that as moms, we too are worthy of investing in self.

Despite the magnetic pull, the inner voice saying *you are here for more*, I felt guilty. Initially my guilt was mostly surrounding my youngest, Arion. Rowan had well over his first year at home with me; Arion did not. They were only in childcare two days a week, four hours each day, but I judged myself so hard for those eight hours. How dare I take away eight hours each week from Arion that I gave to Rowan. Logically I knew Arion was great, and yet I still had this gnawing guilt whispering in my ear that I was somehow fucking up the little one by not spending the exact amount of time with him in his first year as I did with the older one. It was such a weird space to be in because everyone talks about how great it is you are working, but no one talks about how weird it is leaving your kids to do that work.

I felt guilty that I did not want to be a stay-at-home mom. I thought there was something wrong with me because that was not what I wanted, because I wanted to invest time and energy into something other than my children, because I was going against the *shoulds*. For a long time I was in this battle between my ego and my soul.

THE EGO AND THE SOUL

My ego makes herself heard often, every single time my soul is pushing me to my next level. But she has slowly learned to make her regards quietly where she's heard, but not overpowering what my soul is saying. It's a complicated relationship between the soul and the ego, but we make it work because we need both.

Your soul is your connection to the Universe, it is ever expanding. It holds your purpose and your gifts. Without your physical body, your soul could not be on this physical earth sharing your gifts and your light, and you cannot have a physical body without an ego. The ego is not a bad thing, she is here to keep us safe. She just doesn't know the difference between a dinosaur about to have us as a snack, and the fear of stepping out of our comfort zone. It all feels the same to her. So approach her with kindness when she pipes up with her favorite fear reel, she really is just trying to keep you alive. And as we kindly ask her to sit the fuck down and pass the reins to our soul, she adapts, expands and grows. At least until we do the next scary thing, then it's like we are nose-to-nose with a hungry T-Rex all over again.

When we are living from our ego, we are often stuck in fear and resistance. I had a lot of resistance when I considered going back to work after Arion was born. I wasn't only going back to work, I was taking a risk learning something completely new and starting my own business. My ego had a lot to say about it. I was filled with the guilt I mentioned earlier, as well as so much fear. *How could I be any good at this totally new thing when I was already walking in the dark raising these small humans? What if I fail? I probably will fail.* Like my ego believed I couldn't do both: live my purpose and be a kickass mother.

Respectfully ego, fuck yes I can!

So, although my ego was saying I should stay home with my children (ego loves those *shoulds*, they feel safe to her), my soul was shouting just a little bit louder, *let's fucking go. You are here to learn from these boys, you are here to hold space for them and all of their beauty and genius and purpose, and you are also here to show them what it's like to live your purpose. You are here to change the world, and as you do you are opening the doors for them to change the world.*

It is powerful to take notice of when we are living in our ego from a place of fear. The more we create awareness, the more readily we can shift back into soul alignment. When we find ourselves triggered by our children (ie. all the fucking time), for example, we are in ego and we are coming from a place of fear. They trigger us because they are here to teach us. If we can open ourselves up to explore the lesson inside that fear, we can begin to approach our children consciously and shift into a place of soul. When I have the awareness to witness myself in that fear space I use my breath to anchor back into my body. I remove myself from the room (mommy gets time-outs in this house), close my eyes and center myself with three deep breaths, focusing on each inhale and exhale, feeling the breath move through my body. By the third breath I am back in alignment, and I can then respond instead of react.

GETTING TO WORK

When I started training to become a holistic practitioner, I had no clue what I was doing. We couldn't even afford a pumpkin at Halloween, so I definitely was not in a position to be investing in myself, I had to be resourceful. I learned where I could for free, volunteering with mentors, and reading anything I could get my hands on. When I started sending my kids to a babysitter for two half days a week, I had developed enough skills to treat clients for muscle tension and minor soft tissue disorders. I would see a few clients on the first day to pay for the sitter, then spend the rest of the time learning and studying to finish my certification.

Often we hold ourselves back, waiting until we have it all figured out. What I have learned is we don't need to know exactly how we are going to get there, we just need to take the first step. I could have never imagined this is where I would be when I first started out. My business has grown and evolved, and it continues to do so. I am here because I took a leap and opened myself up to possibilities.

BALANCE

How do I balance it all?

Honestly, I don't.

You hear people talk about balance all the time. How does she balance her career and her kids? As if anyone ever asks that of a working dad. Well, here's the truth: balance is a myth. It doesn't exist, at least not in this context. It took me a bit to figure this one out. I was out there trying my hardest to balance this invisible scale: babies, husband, and house on one side, work and soul's purpose on the other. Who knows where fitness or any of the other things fit on this imaginary scale. Think about how ridiculous that is.

For starters, these things are all intertwined. At least in my world. Entrepreneurs, you feel me? But let's say for argument sake, everything is perfectly separate in its own unique categories on either side of the scale. Mine still doesn't balance. I mean I have way more categories than the two sides of the scale for one.

And then of course, at different moments we give more of ourselves to certain areas of our life, whatever is priority in that moment. When I am at the gym, my body and my health are my priority. In the evenings from bus time until bedtime I give my energy to my kids. When I am with my clients, I give my energy to them. And, there may be things that come up that have us investing more in one area than another. For example, when our kids are sick. Or now for instance, I am sitting here writing while my kids are in the other room watching cartoons. Normally the evenings are for them, but with a deadline for this chapter I need to give more here right now, the book is a current priority.

We can never give it all, to all areas equally.
But we believe we should.

We are fighting a losing battle. And because we cannot attain it, now we shame ourselves for it. We tell ourselves how much we are sucking at this mom thing, or that we are failing at work. Ultimately we end up sitting in this pile of mom guilt, shame, and judgement. And, we've piled it on so thick we can't see anything else.

That was me. Drowning in my pile of mom guilt and judgement. Feeling like I failed at all things because I couldn't keep a perfect house and perfect kids while running my perfect business and giving everyone one-hundred percent of me always. Seriously, who created these insanely unrealistic expectations of women? I am happy to say that I have since dug myself out of the guilt pile and stand firm: *fuck the expectations, I'm doing this on my terms. There are no rules.* Now the guilt and the judgement doesn't come as often, and when it does it isn't nearly as loud.

MAMA'S TIME

Once I became more comfortable with working, and the little time I had away from my kids, I then had to figure out where to fit in time just for me, for self care, to fill my cup. And just like that the guilt was back. I thought, how can I take more time for something else when I already take time away from family for my business? Again, I was screaming inside. I was building my business, running the house, and keeping the kids alive, but I was not taking a minute for myself between any of it.

It can be so hard for mamas to create time for ourselves. Whether that is time to go to the gym, time to meditate, time to read, or anything else that fills us up.

As moms we are giving of ourselves constantly; we are giving to our children, our spouses, and our work. But what about us? It's time to get a little selfish in the name of selfless service. It all starts with you, mama. So, fill yourself up first, so you can go out there and continue to kickass at parenting, business, and life. And believe me, regardless of what you think, you are kicking ass.

I had to recognize that just in the way going after my dreams is in fact serving my children, so is taking care of myself. Be gentle with yourself. I recommend getting clear and identifying your *non-negotiables*. These are the things that no matter what you need to do daily, weekly, or monthly to fill your cup. Allow yourself to set those boundaries. For me, daily this included reading, journaling, and meditation. My kids know, if mommy doesn't get meditation time, she is much more likely to turn into a rage-asaurus rex. And that certainly doesn't serve anyone.

These don't have to be lengthy endeavors. It can be as simple as sitting in silence with yourself for one minute. Find the things that feel good for you, and commit that time to yourself.

PURPOSE

There have been a lot of struggles, fear, and guilt along the way, and every bit has been worth it. We are complex divine beings.

We are mom, and we are also so much more.

My work is my passion. It is my soul's purpose to guide people to their greatness: mind, body, and soul. I do this work because of my kids. They allowed me to see myself for all that I am. They showed me I am not meant to passively ride the waves of life finding no true fulfillment. They showed me I am here to share my power, my light, and to create a massive impact on this world. I will keep going. I will continue to move through any guilt, fear, or judgement that arises as I remind myself of why I am here: my purpose.

My boys have been like a roadmap to that purpose. I believe our children are our greatest teachers. They were sent to me to show me the big things I am here to do in this world, to provide me with my greatest lessons, to allow me to grow into my full potential, so I could live out my purpose; while I allow and create space for them to step into their own uniqueness and live their lives of purpose.

I believe it is our job as parents to hold
space for our children to be as they are, to
allow them to explore their genius and own
their purpose.

I believe that when we create space for ourselves to stand in our light and our power, we create space for others. By that nature alone, we are demonstrating so much for our children by allowing ourselves to dig into our purpose and our passions. By investing in our work in this world and going after our dreams, we show our children the magic that comes from doing the work. We show them we can be badass moms and have a massive impact on society at the same time. We show them that there is room for everyone, that our circumstances do not define us, and that we are all worthy of our dreams.

Chapter ten

Just Press Pause

"My attention is my intention."

Michelle Emmick

MICHELLE EMMICK

www.mycoachmd.com
ig: @theplasticsurgerycoach | fb: @My Coach MD
li: Michelle Emmick

Michelle Emmick

Michelle Emmick, known as the Plastic Surgery Coach, is the CEO and Co-founder of MyCoachMD, and an Amazon bestselling author with her debut book *Blue-Collar Beauty*. Michelle has spent close to twenty years in the aesthetics field, having performed over ten thousand patient consultations and working with over three thousand surgeons and support staff. With her mantra of, "Know Before You Go," Michelle saw a need in the market for helping others. Women being so busy, they don't always have time to do all the research, whether that means looking into procedure options or finding the right doctor. Her company not only helps the consumer, Michelle and her colleagues work closely with practices all over the world to provide exceptional patient experiences. They know what excellent service can do for a business, and they make sure that every patient not only looks and feels good, but they would refer their friends and family to that practice. Michelle holds an undergraduate degree in social work and graduate studies in business. Michelle is originally from upstate New York and has spent the last fifteen years in Florida with her husband Mike, daughter Carson, and rescue dog Bailey.

Just Press Pause

Hurry, let's go, we will be late! You can eat breakfast in the car. The late bell rings in seven minutes. Let's goooo!" *Why is getting out of the house so difficult in the morning? I can run a team of hundreds of people, but can't seem to manage this one little person, why is that?*

OK, I have one hour before my first meeting starts, just enough time to fit in a quick workout . . . This is a phone conference, so yes! I can skip the shower and go straight to my desk. I can't afford to lose that precious time. Ah, the life of a work from home mom. The life that provides the freedom to work in your pajamas, makeup free, make your own schedule type of life. Then why do I feel I work more now than I did with an in-office job? That's because, like many women and female business owners and entrepreneurs with a strong type A personality, there is always a new project, new contact, and endless new opportunities to consider.

Oh no, it's 1:45 p.m. I will be stuck in the back of the carline. I just have to send out one more email . . . annnd send! There, I should have enough time; the conference call starts in ten minutes. I'll introduce myself and hit mute. Keys-check, hat—since my hair has yet to see a comb today— check, and out the door while tripping on the dog on my way out. *Oh geez, come on, let's go. You can ride in the back. Oh, now where is my car tag? Ms. Jill will have a fit if it's not there. She needs to see those names of kids going into our cars. She probably knows mine, the hot mess express over here. And of course, it fell between the seats, let me just grab, got it!* All right . . .

"Hi, it's Michelle, just joined!" And Mute. *Ok, please, please, don't ask me any more questions for the next ten minutes. I just need enough time to get my little one into the car, give her a big smile and a ``how was your day'' greeting before the "please be quiet, mommy's on a conference call," or what my daughter is used to seeing, the "don't make a peep look."* I see my daughter's cheery face as she pulls open the car door and throws her backpack in first before plopping down in the backseat. "Oh, come on, you're on the phone?"

I'm sorry, it will just be fifteen minutes, I promise. **Press Pause.**

Cue, the mom guilt. Here I'm thinking, how nice I get to pick my daughter up from school, and yet, I'm too busy to get to appreciate it. This is my life. Probably not different from other work-from-home moms. People have this misconception that if you work from home, you've got it made. I actually think it can be harder. It's not always easy to just stop what you're doing or ignore work. You see an email come through; you know it can wait, but you're right there, it's so easy just to respond and hit a reply—one after the next. And there repeats the cycle. Only one more call, just one more call. My famous last words, "Mommy's almost done."

The fact is, I don't need to answer right away, and quite frankly, it's not even good business to do so. When you are so quick to respond people start expecting it. We're always rushed and stressed and trying to fit in as much as we can in the day. I always say I fit ten hours of work a day into five. When I work, I'm in the zone. I know I'm not alone in this. I've talked to other women that work from home. We don't need to stay connected twenty-four, seven, and yet, that's often what happens, it becomes the norm until something occurs that makes you stop and reevaluate.

"Mom, you promised to take me to the mall to get my picture with Santa today. You said, on Tuesday, we would go to the mall to see Santa. Remember, you said that, and you promised."

I did? Why in God's name did I say that? I'm sure she asked me the exact time I was hopping on a business call. She's a master influencer, my little eight-year-old. As soon as I hop on a call I hear, "Mom, Mom, Mom. Can I have some chips?" I shake my head, No. "Come on, Mom, I didn't have my snack yet." Mean mom's face; another "no" is whispered across the room: "Pleeaasseee Mom, just a few." "Fine, Go!" I'm on a call. Parent of the year over here. I see those Instagram moms having a perfectly plated after-school snack with organic fruits and veggies. My kid is wolfing down from the bag sitting in front of her iPad. I'm a crappy parent. Mom guilt in full effect!

Call completed and off to the mall we go. Ok, this isn't bad, no crowds, no long lines, Mr. and Mrs. Claus are anxiously waiting. This is great. In and out. Smiles, pictures, and candy canes. Mom points on this one for sure. Guilt is subsiding.

"Mom, I brought my gift card Grandma gave me. The store's right there," and she starts walking and pointing. "It's right there Mom!" As she pulls her gift card out of her little flower chain purse and holds it up high. The phone rings.

"Hi, this is Michelle." *Seriously, why do I do this to myself? Why do I pick up the call?* I pick up the phone because my job is to help people. I've made a commitment to support my clients.

"Sure, I'd be happy to help answer your questions," I say to the caller as I see my daughter's eyes light up. Yep, she's got me, right in the palm of her sticky homemade slime hands. I give her the shew, go in front of me into the store. Off we go as she slowly browses for twenty minutes while mom chats away with a client. I watch her pick up every little trinket, with sparkling eyes and smiles and laughter. I love observing the joy she has in life and the things we take for granted. "Look what this does Mom." "I see honey, that's so cool." I'm still on the call as I look down and notice her basket is overflowing. *What in the world?* I give her a raised eyebrow without having to say I think you have exceeded your gift card limit my love. She smiles and shrugs her shoulders. "It's buy three, get three free, Mom."

Sure, of course it is. And the three you buy are the most expensive items. We make it to the register, and she swipes the gift card to reflect a remaining balance of thirty-eight dollars. *You have got to be kidding me! I thought everything in here was like five bucks?* I reluctantly pay the retail worker with a wallet in one hand and my client phone call in the other. My daughter looks up and gives me a side grin. I exchange goodbye pleasantries with the teenage checkout girl and with my super sweet client who has been unknowingly speaking to me while walking in circles around a small retail chain inside the mall.

We make it to the parking lot, put our seat belts on, and my daughter chimes in from the back seat and says thanks mom, that was so fun! I know you're busy with work and I know your job is to help people, so it's ok; they need you too. **Press Pause.** Boy kids are wise. She gets it, but I don't. I missed it. I missed the fact that while yes, the clients I work with need me, so does my daughter, I need to set boundaries so I can be at my best for both.

> *There's a great quote by legendary football coach Tony Dungy that says, "A work ethic that sacrificed family turns out to be all work and no ethic."*

That evening while washing off the cheap makeup and full clown face I allowed her to put on me because of my earlier mom guilt, I realized I'm in over my head. I can't do this. Sure, to the outside, it looks like I'm there, but the fact is I'm not. What am I teaching my child? I don't want to be the mom that's too busy to hear how your day was or enjoy the little experiences. Things need to change. I need a conscious effort to shut down. To be present. **Press Pause.** Let the next call go to voicemail, and email go unanswered.

There is no more important job, and yes, mama has to work, and she also needs to learn to shut down. Slowing down has never been in my makeup. I love to work and always have. I worked so many years inside the corporate bubble and being able to do things now the way

I believe best supports women on their aesthetic journey is beyond fulfilling. I know that what we do makes a difference because with a major life decision, plastic surgery is very personal. My colleagues and I believe it necessary to have someone with you every step of the way for both education and support. I just need to find a better balance to support my clients, my family, and myself.

I wasn't the girl that dreamed of having a family and children. I wanted to work, and then work some more. I was fine watching others with their kids and spending time with my nieces and nephews. My husband felt the same way, and so, we worked—a lot. Then came our amazing surprise. At thirty-eight, my world flipped upside down, for the better, and it left me to figure out how it's done. I forever changed my attention and responsibilities, and now I needed to **Press Pause** to figure out how to get this right. Whatever I do, I want to be good at it, so I took some time to reevaluate and configure our new organizational structure. Just like I had in business or leading a team, I asked myself what changes are needed and what steps need to be in place for our new family dynamic to run at a high level.

I believe there are parallels to our personal and professional lives.

After that day at the mall, I set up some rules. My daughter and I wrote them down together. I wanted to make sure I was teaching her that nobody is perfect, and we are always a work in progress. I want her to know the importance of work ethic and balance. She must know wholeheartedly that she is a priority too. I'm sure there are so many women out there that feel like they are being pulled in many directions. I think the best advice is that we stop being so hard on ourselves and attempt to find balance. Don't be afraid to press pause and put a plan in place to enjoy life. Work isn't going anywhere, but your children are. They are growing up fast, and you don't want to miss the good stuff.

Here are the Press Pause Rules we set up together;

1. Wake up twenty minutes early to sit down and have breakfast together before school.
2. The phone is put down for pick up. No exceptions.
3. One family activity before bed.

Part of putting together the new rules required some additional steps. I had my daughter go to aftercare for a few hours, a few days a week. I knew that for me to adhere to the rules, I needed more time to complete my daily tasks and also have time for myself. On the days I pick her up from school, I have her come into my office. She helps me with projects, and I include her in the work I'm doing when appropriate. I tell her about my day and what I learned just as she does with her day. Scheduling aftercare has given me that extra time to get my work done so that when it is time for pickup, my little peanut has momma's full attention. No distractions, just mom, fully engaged, and happy to share in her day.

The best thing we can do for our children is be present. Your undivided attention means everything.

Kids grow up fast. Whether you work from home, work long hours, or are a stay at home mom, whether you work because you want to or because you have to, as moms, we have a big job in raising smart, happy children. I don't know if there's a perfectly clear path between profession and parenthood. I don't think paths look the same for every mother, but what I believe whether it's running a business or a family, taking the time to self-reflect, evaluate what's working and what isn't, and getting some clarity on what's important to you, can make the difference. Setting rules can help minimize the craziness, provide a clear focus, and maybe, just maybe eliminate a little of that mommy guilt. I'm not naïve to believe that I've got it figured out, and as I say to the clients I coach and my daughter, we should always learn and grow, to better ourselves. To do this, everyone once in a while take the time to **Press Pause.**

Section three

True Fulfillment:
Trials and Triumphs

FEATURING:

Teresa Nocita
Domenica Orlando
Melissa Killeleagh
Andie Mack
Nanci Lozano

Chapter Eleven

All You Need Is Love

"You can choose to focus on and complain about the shitty parts of your life, but if you change nothing, nothing changes. There's no loss in going for it!"

Teresa Nocita

TERESA NOCITA

www.thevocalcompass.com
ig: @teresanocita | fb: @teresa nocita | t: @teresanocita

Teresa Nocita

Teresa Nocita has been coaching developing vocal artists as a vocal coach in Canada and the United States since the 1990s. She has over thirty years of vocal training including studies at Boston's Berklee College of Music. In addition to being an accomplished musician, she has also studied to become a reiki master and certified yoga instructor and now an author, since developing a revolutionary "yoga for the voice technique" and stamping it in a book called *The Vocal Compass*™, she's been in demand throughout the music, voice, and health industry. Teresa's book *The Vocal Compass*™, has been a bestseller at Canadian Music Week, as well as other platforms that she has spoken at across Canada and the USA. Teresa is releasing her second edition of *The Vocal Compass*™ in 2020, and is endorsed by the Ontario Music Therapists Association. She's the owner and director of Studio E Music and Arts, a creative environment arts school with over five hundred students and twenty-five employees. Anyone using their voice professionally is excited about the simple, revolutionary technique that Teresa provides. Teresa lives just outside of Toronto, Ontario.

All You Need Is Love

It was sometime during the summer of 2006; in the middle of the night . . . I tried, I tried really hard. Something inside me just wouldn't allow me to pick up my screaming baby to rock her, soothe her, feed her; mother her. Why? Well, how could I pick her up? Touch her. I had bugs crawling all over me, they would spread . . . The bugs would transfer to my screaming baby. My husband asked in the moment, "What's wrong? Why aren't you taking care of our crying baby?" I convincingly, in hysterics, responded that I had been infested, that bugs were crawling all over me! Disgusting, infesting bugs. I repeatedly asked my husband to check my skin, my head, the pillows, and the bed sheets. His answer: "YOU'RE CRAZY, go take a shower, take something."

So I did something, seven months later, for my diagnosed postpartum psychosis. A crippling, mental state of hallucination is what I had been experiencing from hormones, stress, and thoughts. They were so real; I was terrified, and I didn't know what was happening, or even how to deal with it.

At this point I had been married for four years and had one child that was three years old, and one an infant. I was twenty-seven years old. I ended up seeing postpartum specialists and a postpartum nurse three to five days a week for about two years at the St. Joseph's Mental health clinic in town. They had me try many medications and different doses to find which one would help me, or even to keep me alive. My ex-husband hadn't the slightest idea to the extent of what I was feeling or going through on a daily basis, and frankly, he avoided it. I was alone; or at least I felt alone. I was choosing to believe that you just get dealt a bad hand, and when the bad luck ran out, the problems would somehow disappear and they'll go away. Well, they did with the medication, temporarily, until I went back to work. Those darn bugs came back, and I needed to protect myself and my children from these bugs. The hallucinations were also paired with anxiety, depression, GERD, phobias, and OCD. Once I was on the right medication and was stable, I felt back to myself, until I found out in 2008 that I was pregnant with my third baby. And so it began again . . .

* * *

Okay. Enough of that. When I started to write this, I wanted to share all of my struggles and shortfalls so you can feel you're not alone, and I fell into the old habit of negativity, and it felt gross. What is it with us wanting to fall into the negative spiral of wanting and needing a victim mentality? Entrepreneur, author, and influencer Gary Vaynerchuk says, "People want the benefits, but aren't willing to accept the sacrifices. Want special things? It takes special effort."

You can choose to focus on and complain about the shitty parts of your life, but if you change nothing, nothing changes. There's no loss in going for it!

I am going for it, and changing the focus of this chapter and saying enough pity party! I will trust my gut even though everyone wants to know about everyone else's failures. People are much more interested in people's struggles than their successes. I choose to change that; we NEED and MUST change that. It has been my journey's destination to focus on the positive rather than focus on the negative. I had created a negative environment, getting married too young at the age of twenty-three, having a child within the first year, and ultimately divorced. Even though I may not have been in the right emotional state for all these life changes to happen the way they did, I've decided to move forward and make better choices now.

Forty-two years of ups and downs; way more downs, than ups. It was no wonder I had thoughts of suicide on more than a few occasions. I am forty-two, and I am alive, more alive than ever. I am vibrant, thriving, strong, determined, fearless (for the most part), and most importantly, loved! I am loved and supported unconditionally by my current partner and my children. I know now that the right partner that loves and supports you makes a world of difference. One that chooses to grow with you, and has the same values and beliefs as you, and in you. I have all of this now because I choose and feel that I am deserving.

My current success is the result of the long, excruciating, gruelling, intensely painful, and healing journey that began ten years ago, when I decided to see the first of my three most influential spiritual energy healers. I was fed up. I didn't want to be afraid anymore.

Conventional western medicine was not working for me. I chose to research and try alternative treatments, anything that would help me. I knew there was more.

There was a way to heal myself, to understand how my body was reacting to my thoughts and environment.

My expectation was that I would be instantly healed, just like that. On the contrary, the first visit with my first healer was the first of many, many visits towards my external and internal self-discovery. A new belief system, a new way of thinking, of doing, of observing, and of living. At that first appointment, the words that stood out (and I now hold myself accountable for everyday) were "come from a place of love." *A place of love? What the fuck was that?* At that moment, a world I had never known hit me like a ton of bricks. I didn't know what love was. . . How? I'm a daughter, a sister, a wife, a human being, A MOTHER!

What I had realized was that there was love around me, but I was unable to love myself unconditionally, or I was choosing not to love myself unconditionally; and in turn couldn't love or receive love from others. I was reactive, judgemental, fearful, self sabotaging; not only to myself, but to others. I was holding negativity, a lot of it, which was causing inflammation and chaos in my body. What I thought was being done to me, is what I was doing to myself. How and what did I need to do to come from a place of love? That was a loaded question. That first healer basically summed up the pure essence of life for me. I had reiki treatments, past life regressions, hypnosis, downloads, cord cuttings, clearings, and used plenty of sage and stones that would help me find the first little bit of me, who I was, and what I wanted to become. I still had a lot of work to do.

The next healer I worked with to move forward was a beautiful clairvoyant, one that channels through other dimensions and speaks to guides, my guides. She was influential to me because she is the one that held me accountable for doing the work. My spirits wanted me to write, a lot! I was given assignments to journal and write affirmations. "I love myself," "I am powerful," "I am pure," "I am love," "I am worthy."

Anything I wanted or needed to be or focus on, I would write over and over again.

Other affirmations effective for me were: *As I am in alignment, my family is in alignment; Every challenge creates a lesson learned; As I learn my own lessons, I allow others to learn theirs; I have all the control I need*; and, *As I let go of control, I let go of stress.* Before I ate, I would write an affirmation such as: *The food I choose to eat will nourish my body*, over and over again, so I wouldn't react to the food I was eating. The reaction was from anxiety and fear. The fears slowly dissipated. When I wrote, I felt it to be real! I went through notebooks like diapers! I made my weekly visits to Indigo to buy the most inspiring notebooks to write in.

I knew it wasn't enough. My thoughts would always go back to the negative side. I was still suffering, physically, and mentally. I continued to do the work, but why wasn't I feeling *normal*? Again, I was fed up. I was losing hope.

Until one day, I was out shopping, and the sales lady looked at me with a concerned look and said to me, "Are you ok? You look sad." I broke down, right there, in the middle of their showroom. I couldn't speak. How and why was I breaking down? I had done so much work for myself to get better. Why?! She then pulled out a piece of paper and a pen and wrote a number down for me, and said call this woman, she will help you.

Desperately, I called her. A holistic medical coach, combined with energy healing, reflexology, clairvoyance, and much more. I called her The Wizard. She knew everything. She knew what I was going through, and what I needed to do for myself to move forward, so much that she healed my acid reflux in that first phone call! I still work with this healer to this very day—not as often—but I call her when I feel that I need help to work through something to continue to move forward. She has taught me to write and acknowledge my negativity, and change the habits. She has opened my eyes to a world of healing myself through the acknowledgment of emotions and how they connect physically, and then changing it with the processing and choice of thoughts, choosing the thoughts that serve me rather than the thoughts that don't. She balances my body through reflexology and most importantly, calls me out on my shit.

After all these years, and all this self-discovery and hard work (many hills and valleys), I can honestly say I'm in the best place, mentally, that I have ever been in my life, this far.

I am now able to rewire the way I think to reflect my positive outlook when noticing that I have had a thought that doesn't serve me in a positive way. I have been able to stop filling voids with material items such as cars, houses, clothes, etc. I have chosen to only look for approval and validation from myself, and not from others. I have chosen to love myself and others unconditionally, and live in the moment. To form my own opinion, and not take on other's opinion of me. To pay attention to my breath to bring me back to the moment. I am able to make a list of what needs to be done in my life, and remove myself from it to live in the moment.

Having made some very difficult, life changing choices like leaving my first husband and my home, I've had to choose not to take on what people say about me, as I am the only one that knows what's right for me, and what feels good in my body, my mind, and in my heart. This is what I urge anyone to do. Find what's right and what works for you. Everyone is different.

Being in a great place mentally and physically, I still don't have all the answers for every obstacle, and that's ok. You have to do what's best for you and explore your options according to what you need at that moment in time. I choose happy, calm, confident, strong, brave, positivity and love . . . I CHOOSE LOVE. I needed love in my moment of moving forward. I finally realized that any emotion you choose to hold, you can feel and find inside yourself, in your mind and in your heart, and solely for yourself. Choosing what you want to feel can create the life you choose to live. When thinking positively, you train your mind and heart to feel enlightenment and bliss, *if* you choose that that is what you need for yourself. Each and everyone of us holds the power to rewire and change our thought process to change how we feel. Only we ourselves can take on negativity, which means that you are holding negativity for yourself (the law of attraction). It started with choosing LOVE for me. When holding on to a positive intention such as love, your body exudes, spreads, and spills that positive intention, love, into every other part of your life, including into all your relationships. Therefore, receiving love! Holding a positive intention for yourself can be powerful.

I am love, therefore, I am loved.

As a working mom and entrepreneur, I have chosen to hold the intention of love, confidence, worthiness, self honor, and calm about balancing my personal and professional life. I wake up and hold intentions everyday, for me, my children, and my spouse; my family. These are the intentions I hold when I drive, shop, and have fun, even as I am writing this! This allows the possibility of integrity, growth, health, and abundance. I am repaid with the same with fulfillment, and what I hold comes back to me tenfold because that is what I choose.

I choose to be the best mom I can be, not the perfect one. Side note: There is no such thing as perfect.

I choose to be the best partner, the best sister, the best boss, the best daughter. At times this may even mean in order to be the best you can be, you would need to choose not to be anyone of those at all and remove yourself completely!

As you are aware, I have mentioned the word "choose" a ton in this chapter, and if you did, GOOD—I got my point across! YOU and only YOU have the ability to choose and navigate your own life. Want a better life? CHOOSE to change it! Do something about it! You can do this! Thinking and doing are very different. You can think about saving money or getting into better shape (that's the easy part). But actually digging deep, and rolling up your sleeves to put in the work, is the part we all struggle with the most.We have to understand that life is difficult and nothing happens overnight. On average, we live a life of seventy-five years; that is plenty of time to fulfill most of our goals, but why do we want to have everything accomplished in two minutes flat? Set small goals even if it takes a year. That year will pass you by whether or not you do something to change. Choose to take action! I've been on my self-discovery journey for ten years now, ultimately working towards choosing to focus on me, so that at the end of day I can rest knowing that I did the very best of my ability at that moment in my life.

Being a working person is simply a difficult task on the best days, add the MOM part in there, and we have a completely different recipe—with the same ingredients and instructions. I choose for you, dear reader, that I have inspired you to carry on, to celebrate you and all you have chosen, minute by minute, day by day. May love and light be with you on your journey.

Chapter twelve

Bringing it Back to the Basics: Love and Passion

"Life will present to you stories; you can just mindlessly read them over, or, you can act them out with your full being and experience, all the feelings and emotions for each and every story; choose wisely."

Domenica Orlando

DOMENICA ORLANDO

https://www.familyconnectionscollective.com
ig: @i.am.domenica
fb: @domenicaorlando2 | @family.connections.collective

Domenica Orlando

Domenica Orlando, a mom, boss, wife, daughter, sister, aunt, friend, community creator, problem solver, miracle worker, dreamer, lover of life resides in Burlington, Ontario with her two babies, husband, and their beloved pug. Domenica is thirty five years old and is a mental health advocate primarily for mothers and women suffering in silence with their mental illness. Her advocacy began when Domenica had experienced postpartum depression following her daughter's birth. Ending the stigma and speaking the secret drove Domenica to use her voice and create an online community based on acceptance, adversity, and support. As mentioned Domenica wears many hats like a lot of women do, she plans and executes a variety of events in and around the Halton region. Empowering women, catering to the family unit, and showing her appreciation of small and local businesses drives Domenica's event collective. Domenica began her career in education after graduating from Ryerson University. She completed her Masters of Arts degree in Early Childhood Studies and then received her bachelors in primary education from the University of Ontario. You can find Domenica either enjoying a coffee and networking with fellow Burlington mompreneurs, planning an event, or enjoying down time with her favorite people, her family.

I asked myself throughout writing this chapter, what do I want my audience to take away after reading it? And I reiterated to myself, it *has* to be relatable to the average woman, or mama, I mean that's how I conduct myself within my online community, but the truth is, not everyone will relate to you and you have to be okay with that. This was a great practice to let go of my previous thoughts, insecurities, feelings, and emotions, and allow myself to speak from the heart without hesitation.

Mama's, ladies, to whomever is reading this, I want you to leave feeling motivated, ready to tackle the next steps in your journey, and maybe leave a little trail of enlightenment to push forward! I'm sharing some vulnerable stuff here, some of these things I've only said to myself, they have yet made their debut to the outside world, so consider yourself special.

I'll give you a glimpse as to what *work* means to me, and let me tell you, I have a strong feeling there will be many of you saying to yourself "me too," or "can I get an amen" (or at least I hope so). I want you to feel my emotions through my words and I hope they put some fire under your butt to get up and *run* towards your dreams!

THE BEGINNING OF THE END, OR SO I THOUGHT . . . JULY 2, 2016.

Life as I knew it was *gone*, feelings of loneliness, regret rushed through me as if an ocean wave had crushed my bones and my lively, bubbly spirit just drifted away. My daughter was born on this day. The minute I held her I felt hatred towards myself. Not her, no, see, I loved her, I immediately felt *bad* for her because she had *me* as a mother. I wanted to scream, I wanted to tell someone, *anyone,* that I wanted to escape. I wanted to run away and not look back, but everyone kept asking me, "Are you going to breastfeed?" and, "Are you in pain?" I would just cry when I looked at her, scared out of my mind and continually asking myself, *how on earth am I going to raise this human being when I can't even get my own crap together.* I was doomed. I didn't want to leave the hospital because that just meant I had to *do life* with this tiny baby.

My husband was working crazy hours, poor guy, he wasn't around, and it was not his fault—he tried, the look in his eyes when he would watch me cry, ripped me apart. This man had to "deal" with his sick wife plus the baby; I apologized profusely and told him to leave me as I was a terrible excuse of a spouse and now mother. This was motherhood as I knew it. There were no rosey, blissful moments with my child. I saw darkness. I saw a tunnel, a hole, the worst part of it all, I saw *no end in sight*. Motherhood was robbed from me, I began building resentment towards *all mothers* who seemed happy, who did not want to get to know me because I was *different* or at least they made me feel this way. I felt disconnected from the world. It was lonely and isolating for me.

As the days and months went by, I opened up to people and used my online platform to speak about my mental health, and also to help and advocate for those women suffering in silence.

I felt for the first time in my life I was making a difference; I felt ful-filled. I felt as though that I might have found my new passion: helping and serving people. In the beginning there was a ton of love and com-passion towards my story with postpartum depression, however one day I experienced the harsh reality of the repercussions of sharing your truth online with complete strangers. It was not love; it was not compas-sion; it was not a reflection of how women should be acting towards each other. However, this is the risk you take when you put yourself out there publicly. We will not be relatable to every woman, therefore we need to just be true to ourselves and as authentic as possible. I allowed adversity to fuel me; I did not allow it to set me back, nope. If anything, it pushed me so far forward that I made it my sole-purpose to advocate for the silenced and oppressed.

NEW OUTLOOK, NEW PURPOSE, NEW MEANING . . . BUT FOR HOW LONG?

Fast forward to fourteen months postpartum, I began my journey with medication; I continued my sessions with my therapist, and I be-gan feeling like myself again. Seeking acceptance from those around me stopped a long time prior, and I was on my fresh path towards self-discovery.

Domenica Orlando

Mama was ready to head back to work,
or so I thought.

First month back at the post-secondary institution I was teaching at, I felt a sense of loss. Constantly questioning my existence in my role as an educator. I was certain I was making a difference in my student's lives, however I did not feel this, I felt as though I had to do *more* for my community. I still wanted to work because it brought me independence, purpose, meaning to my life, but I felt empty. I experienced a turning point. I wanted to create a career around helping people succeed, rediscovering themselves whether it be professionally, personally, spiritually, or soulfully.

I began coaching. I found myself a mentor, and I delved into the world of intention, mindfulness, and gratitude. I felt as though I was at peace with myself and had forgiven myself for all the guilt from the depression. Truth is, this was a turning point in my life, I felt good, however I allowed it to slip away and looking at it now, I can't help but think how different my life would have been. All the hard work I did on soul searching, I was losing it, I moved further and further away from my clients mentally, spiritually, and emotionally; and I devoted my time to gaining an online presence based on influencing. I also began working in corporate events, predominantly within GTA malls. There was always so much pressure put on the organizers to create perfection for their audience. Looking back, I was not in my comfort zone. I delved into a whole new persona, someone trying to portray and uphold this identity to the outside world that was not authentic and transparent.

When we talk about work and what it means to every one of us, I never saw work as desperate—something that I *needed*! However, the meaning changed, and the desperation had surfaced so quickly I could not get a hold of it. I felt as though I was headed down that path again of isolation, darkness, and loneliness. I allowed the "gram" to take over my thoughts and actions, I had allowed complete strangers and groups of people to dictate my actions going forward.

Looking back I am embarrassed. Embarrassed that I allowed money, popularity, gifts, and fame to take over my mindset. My mind at this point was filled with *ego,* and that's not a comfortable place to be. In hindsight, I was not in a positive spot. But that's what happens when you allow desperation to settle in. Everyone was trying to be somebody. My God, it was all about competition, and the more individuals would jump on the bandwagon of "community over competition" were in fact so far from that reality.

Our events had to be the best looking, the brighter lights, better vendors, bigger balloons, *what was this all for?* Was it for accolades from our peers? From complete strangers? Personally, it was for a sense of pride, however, our peers did not truthfully care. Let's be honest, people do not like it when you pass them on that ladder. They do not want to see you doing better than them, they are uncomfortable with your success.

I questioned everything; my purpose, my own intentions, and the intentions of those around me.

Don't misconstrue my words, I enjoyed working, I craved the rush and adrenaline from the events. But, work wasn't cutting it anymore, I needed more, both my husband and I had agreed we desperately needed a change. So, we decided to pack up and move cities! Burlington, Ontario, here we come!

REBIRTH, RENEW, AND RECONSTRUCT

I was excited for our life in Burlington: new vibes, new neighbourhood, people, and a brand-new community! I wanted to bring my work to Burlington andOakville, and I was so happy to be in a new place. My heart, soul, and mind were at ease.

I turned to passion and love. But before I reached that plateau of serenity, I'd have to experience some storms along the way.

This move saved me and was so crucial for my overall wellbeing. I didn't know it, but my foundation aka: my spiritual soul was cracked. I had reached a fork in the road and a storm was brewing, but remember, not all storms come to disrupt our journey, they sometimes come through to wash out what needs to vanish. I didn't know who the hell I was anymore. 2019 was a year of re-birth, my re-birth.

Beginning of the year I was mid-way through my pregnancy, busy renovating our home, settling my little one in daycare, and the feeling of isolation had hit me and my depression and anxiety were heightened. An incident occurred in and around this time, it happened online; it shook me and broke me. I was being bullied and threatened by an individual regarding some false accusations, the severity of the stress had almost put me in the hospital. I have since healed and moved on from it, however, it is something that played a vital role in why I am in the position I am in today. Following this incident I lost faith in humanity. My trust with people did not exist, I lost touch with my spirituality and what made my soul happy. Rather than using this to fuel me and my business to strive forward, I allowed it to break me. I was so worried about my pregnancy and my mental health that it consumed me to the point where I began to hide from people. I was in fact broken.

Following the birth of my son in June, something came over me, I was exhausted from hiding. I was sick of being mad and angry, and giving so much emotion to individuals that did not deserve to take up any real estate in my soul. I had my ah-ha moment and I no longer felt trapped, but liberated to strive forward. I made a promise to myself to never go back to being a slave to social media or use it for my capital gain. I was just tired of selling on the gram, and trying to convince people of things. I wanted to inspire and empower women to make their own choices and decisions, rather than just listen and follow me. Making real-life relationships with people, and living in the moment, was more of my jam.

I promised myself to never feel victimized,
and to use my platform to empower and
inspire women to speak their truth, own their
decisions, and share their vulnerabilities.

Work began to look a little different by the end of 2019. I went off on my own, and created a brand-new events company. My goal was to create a community, one gathering at a time. I wanted to bring my experiences in life and soul coaching to the events collective, and help as many vendors as possible to expand their business, all while being as relatable as possible. I felt as though I found my place again, I was going back to the basics, my passion for people, the place I call home. You see, work for me, is not and will not be a final destination, it's forever evolving. It's a place of growth, and inspiration. I organize events to empower women, business owners, and individuals within our community. Since moving to Burlington, my focal point with work has been community and growth. Stepping out of your comfort zone will take you places where you've never imagined. Everyone works, it's what you do with it that makes it special.

I crave it, I want it, and that's why this Mama's gotta work!

Chapter thirteen

Sometimes Having an Affair Is the Only Answer . . .

"When all I want is that love and affection, and I just can't get enough, a girl's gotta do what a girl's gotta do."

Melissa L. Killeleagh

MELISSA L. KILLELEAGH

ig: @flxmelissak | fb: @melissa.killeleagh | li: melissa killeleagh

Melissa L. Killeleagh

I'm not really into titles, but the best one for me would be mompreneur. I am blessed to be building a business around my almost four-year-old son Jack and my commitments to our community here in the Fingerlakes region of upstate New York. Born and raised in Buffalo, NY, I did most of my growing up in both Ithaca and Binghamton, where I completed my undergraduate and graduate degrees. With some travel and a term in Americorps sprinkled in, I followed a fairly expected trajectory for my life early on. After a ten-year career in finance, and when stress had gotten the best of me, I retired myself from the nine to five in an attempt to stop racing through the length of my life, and start embracing the fullness of it. With over thirteen years in network marketing, my journey is all about values driven living and creating a life that doesn't just look good from the outside, but feels amazing from the inside. Building that life while becoming a mom and living on my own hasn't been easy, but it has always been worth it. I had to develop my own inner GPS to truly fall in love with the journey and love everything that keeps me connected spiritually, whether it's exploring with my son, hiking our gorges, doing yoga, reading a great book, or having coffee and a conversation with a great friend. I love sharing stories of people living their lives with passion and purpose on my podcast @themelissakilleleaghshow and I'm beyond thrilled to be part of the collaboration that is *Mama's Gotta Work*.

Sometimes Having an Affair Is the Only Answer . . .

Before we begin, I will warn you that my friends often call me old-fashioned. They also say that I'm an old soul. I'm hoping that before the end of our time together here, you might want to be one of those friends. So, while I may share some thoughts that trigger you, especially if you're a *one-way only* kinda progressive, I'm crossing my fingers that you can forge ahead with an open heart and mind, and join me on this journey, hopefully judgment free.

So, where do I begin? In the beginning, of course! Only I don't know where or when that is. What I *do* know is when that plus sign appeared, some things became crystal clear. Everything I never knew for sure I wanted, but was told I'd likely never have (thank you, undiagnosed celiac disease and years of unexplained infertility), and therefore knew I MUST HAVE, was now suddenly a very real, exciting—and *terrifying*—possibility. The tidal wave of emotions was just the beginning of the roller-coaster ride I was getting on.

Almost five years later, as I sit here writing this, I'm pretty sure I'm still riding it! Every twist and turn has brought both blessings and lessons. Jack's laughter at four years old, is my cue to celebrate every moment. While many of my friends set sail on the quest for perfect parenting (books, blogs, and podcasts galore), I decided from day one that this little one was here to teach me some very important lessons in this life. And he has. Including knowing when it was time to pursue that affair you will be learning about. Just don't judge me . . . yet. It's hard to believe that something so pure and so perfect could drive me to do something so drastic.

"The heart wants what the heart wants." -Emily Dickinson

Everything was picture perfect. We met in the fall, on a day when the sun filtered through the windows in such a way you might wonder whether it would ever fade. His smile was reserved, and yet, oddly reassuring. I knew we would meet again. He owned his business, as I did mine, and seemed supportive of the lifestyle required of an entrepreneur. From the storefront of his building, you could watch the world pass by and I felt his eyes follow me as I slipped away into that sunny day.

Several months later, we were living together and when I was home, we cocooned into the bliss common to the beginning of any relationship. It was a new year *and* my first year as a solo business owner. I was excited to explore the world—from Costa Rica to Mexico, and Las Vegas—and I was also on an intense inner journey, as I learned more about what my heart had been longing for all those years of working the nine to five grind. Truth be told, I had *a lot* of work to do because my "hustle for worthiness" began long before I entered the working world, starting with getting good grades, performing as if I was always on stage, and seeking the approval of anyone and everyone around me.

Let's just say that the affair I'd eventually have—and will certainly never regret—is one that even the most clueless sleuth could have foreshadowed back then. I was determined to prove my worth and let's be honest, love is one of the easiest ways to do that. The first time you hear those words "I love you" and everything feels right in the world, you realize how powerless you are to that intoxicating emotion. And listen, when all you want is that love and affection (anyone else hearing the Nelson twins singing right now? I totally just gave away my age), and you just can't get enough, a girl's gotta do what a girl's gotta do.

Sometimes the only answer is to have the
wildest, world rocking, love affair of your life.

By the time I figured all of this out, I was probably about four months into my pregnancy and rocking my Richard Simmons "Sweatin' to the Oldies" wristbands (ok, they were sea bands for acupressure). I was some shade of green on even my best days, my feet had already grown a half size from the ten I was already in, and I was very visibly pregnant. Who would want me looking like this? In no time at all, I lost sight of my feet entirely. The cause seemed hopeless. It would seem that drastic times would call for drastic measures. Manifesting what you want requires taking action (little known fact for all you followers of the *Law of Attraction*), so I booked the most beautiful suite I could find at a historical Bed and Breakfast with a good-sized jacuzzi. There I was, ready to experience the depth and fullness of the love I'd been longing for . . .

LET THIS LOVE AFFAIR BEGIN!

By now, I'm sure you're no longer wondering with whom I'd chosen to share that special evening! The most qualified lover I could find at the time. ME! In case you hadn't already caught on. The wildest, world rocking, love affair of your life is with the lead in your story, the captain of your journey—YOU! If this is not already crystal clear to you, take note immediately: there is not one person on this planet more qualified to love the f#$% out of you than *you!* Many of us don't learn this until motherhood, if even then, and often we give so much of ourselves and our love to our children, that the love affair ends before it ever truly begins.

If you're anything like me, love has often been something I sought from others . . . family and friends, boyfriends, and lovers. I could hardly seem to get enough. It was the cup I could never seem to keep filled. Eventually I learned two important lessons: one, it's not about what we get, but what we give. The more we love, the more love there is. From what I hear, this is often the discovery when you have a second child, having wondered how you'll possibly love the second as much as the first. Two, like Rachel Hollis' analogy on how we show up and show our love in the world—just like the cup I couldn't keep filled—she says we are like vases constantly tipping over to pour into others.

If we stand still and tall and pour into ourselves, we have no option but to eventually overflow into everyone and everything around us.

In this way, I no longer recognized *self-love* as a thing. There is simply love. When we start with ourselves, we become love. We radiate love. And the cup is *always* full. Now, don't get me wrong, I am not a perfect example of what this looks like. Like yoga and meditation, this is a life-long practice. It is the practice of radical self-care. I'm not talking about the luxurious monthly spa day or the token mani-pedi appointment you don't have time for at the moment, or even dinner and dancing with your girlfriends on a Friday night (all of which I highly recommend, however). This affair is on your calendar every day—non-negotiable—and is so simple you might overlook it.

GET BACK TO THE BASICS

I don't know about you, but my pregnancy was both a boot camp for mastering the mundane and surrendering into a deep relationship to the divine. I realized at a certain point that with all-day sickness (congratulations to those of you who only experience this in the morning!) and an everlasting roller-coaster of hormones and emotions, survival depended on how well I could care for this home I'd been given and was now sharing. A few rules prevailed during this difficult time that carried forward into the present, paving the path of not only a healthy life, but a thriving business. Because guess what?! You guessed it—mama's gotta work!

1. Fuel yourself for performance.

This one was tricky during most of my pregnancy. I might have opted for a pint of peanut butter cup ice cream at every meal, but soon I saw the impact of caving to my cravings. My son's father declared to the doctor—in my defense—that I was "all baby." Her response: "in all of her years in delivery, she'd never seen a sixty five pound baby." I decided at that point to choose foods that fueled me. I opted for an anti-inflammatory approach—eliminating common allergens entirely, and since I was already gluten-free, this translated into a power-packed, high-protein, mostly plant-based, whole food diet. Ultimately, let the foods you choose be the gifts you bring to this home for this long-term trip around the sun. I've mostly continued this regimen, and it continues to serve me well.

2. Pay attention to how you spend, or invest your time.

Our calendars (and checkbooks) reflect the values we live by. A quick study will reveal whether you are living your values. For much of my life, I was out of alignment, and not only that, I spent significant time on tasks that didn't really matter. Pregnancy allowed me to slow down (whether I liked it or not), see clearly, and bring my life into alignment with what mattered most to me. I surrendered, and in doing so, I stepped into the flow of a fast-moving stream of a well-lived life. I was in my happy place if I was napping, tapped into nature, or plugged into people who lit me up from the inside out. When we invest our time into that which brings us the greatest joy, life affords us much more ease and grace.

3. Mind your mind.

Just like the quality of the food we put in our mouths reflects our love for our *home* and affects how well it serves us, our minds need us to feed them with good thoughts. Choosing loving and supportive thoughts over nitpicking the things you forgot or didn't get to on your never-ending list will serve you better as you juggle priorities. We hear frequently how thoughts become things, and it couldn't be more true that we become a living reflection of everything we think about. If you could use some help here, one of my favorite friends in the self-talk sector is Dr. Shad Helmstetter. His work set my life onto an entirely new trajectory!

CHANGE YOUR THOUGHTS, CHANGE YOUR LIFE

Shortly after my son was born, our circumstances changed. Jack and I moved out on our own into a loft apartment one town away from his father, and I began negotiating the territory of single parenting. For me, it was easy to get defeated feeling like I didn't have a lot of resources—my closest family were hours away and financially, I hadn't planned for this. However, just like I'd always heard, the teacher appears when the student is ready to learn. One day this appeared as I looked into the mirror, written in bold across my mind: I would always have myself, and despite this precious little human lying in my arms, the relationship to myself was still the most important one. Motherhood is an act of love in and of itself but when our love lives outside of ourselves, we will simply never have or be or do enough. When our children become the object of our love, we can often feel empty and unfulfilled and not know why. When you're tired and running on fumes, it is easy to get frustrated and even resentful with so much to *do*. Love is a verb, but I think we often get it wrong. While the realization may seem complex, it was a simple shift that unlocked a whole new world: it is not so much about what we are doing in as much as it is about who we are being while we are doing it. I began to use love as the lens through which I did everything, from making my power-packed morning smoothies to cuddling inside of my favorite cozy sweater, responding to my son's never-ending needs, and showering my body with love (when I could actually get a shower, that is).

Everything has the potential to become an
even better expression of love.

Even my systems and routines became part of it. I forced myself for many months—until it just became natural—to get myself out of bed before my son (often before THE sun!) to focus on the quality of my inner world. I practiced Hal Elrod's life-**s**avers acronym (from his book, *The Miracle Morning*) starting with a minute each and working my way up to what became my honor hour every morning: enjoying the **s**ilence so needed, but rarely afforded; **a**ffirming love into my life and myself; **v**isualizing what my ideal day would look like; **e**xercising; **r**eading; and **s**cribing—reflection is one of our most transformative tools.

These simple acts become even more powerful when practiced over time. It's like experiencing the impact of compound interest, only it applies to the state of your mind. When you start the day racing out of bed like there's a fire in the house, eventually you'll burn out. However, when you prioritize the time to guard your mind, you'll find your foundation stronger than ever.

SHAKE YOUR MONEY MAKER

Shifting myself to this kind of radical self-care required me to work from the inside out. Minding my mind and working on my inner world came first for me because this human *being* needed to learn how to not fall back into the trap of human *doing*. With my son Jack on my back, I started having dance parties in the kitchen during our Monday meal prep sessions, walking to the farmer's market to get our groceries, and even found a mommy and me yoga class.

Motion not only creates e-motion, it also allows you to express it and release it.

Moving my body became both a personal priority for my physical, mental, and emotional health, and it also became a simple way to connect with others and create community again. I established some of my favorite friendships of my life (imagine that, in my forties) while playing in the park with other moms and kids, and over coffee walks while my son napped in his stroller. What will work for you might differ greatly from what worked for me, so I leave you with these questions to spark some solutions for your journey:

What are your top values?

What brings you joy?

What does life look like right now?

When you get in touch with what truly moves you in life, your inner GPS will keep you on track living a life that feels more fulfilling.

SHIFT HAPPENS

Even with the best of intentions, during the first few years after my son's birth, I found myself back in a trap of surviving from nap to nap. Between late nights working on my business and when I wasn't consistently working on myself, I lost the spark. What I failed to realize is that self-care, and our relationship to ourselves, like parenting, is a lifelong commitment. Read that again. Sometimes we are so busy racing from one thing to the next, getting through the length of our life, that we miss out on experiencing the depth and width of it. I was determined to stop just getting by, and start thriving again.

> *"Don't ask what the world needs. Ask what makes you come alive, and go do it. Because what the world needs is people who have come alive."*
>
> -Howard Thurman

I asked myself the very question I asked when I decided to move out on my own when my son was born: how do I want my days and my life to *feel*? Only I knew the answer, just like you are the only one who can answer for you. And if you want to dig really deep in this personal excavation, answer the question with all of your senses. Notice the moments that take your breath away: the feel of the breeze on your skin on a warm summer day, the way light shines through the trees and through the window, the sound of your child's laughter, the smell of their skin. Take it all in. Then use it to create more of what matters to you.

The real shift happened for me when I realized that I'd lost touch with focusing on what my son was experiencing, and that as I fill my own cup and have even more love to give, I can also lean in and let this little teacher of mine tell me how he wants to feel and what makes him come alive. Recently, we started practicing Ho'oponopono at home, and this ancient Hawaiian practice has transformed the love within and between us.

IT TAKES A VILLAGE

As I ventured along on this value-driven journey, it occurred to me that the *village* we need isn't simply to raise the child. We all benefit by surrounding ourselves with other people, especially mamas, who also know that this journey isn't always an easy one, who welcome being real about it, and who challenge themselves to live, love, and parent consciously. These aren't always the people we grew up with, or even our families.

It isn't always easy, but it is always worth it.

Assemble your village full of human beings, not human doings, who are living out the width and depth of their years, and learning to love themselves so deeply that they have no option but to be love and pour love into everyone and everything around them—that is my real love affair these days and what led me here to you! I hope you'll choose to build your village too. It starts with you, and the greatest love affair you'll ever have. Once you love yourself in that deep, delicious way, you'll undoubtedly attract even more of that into your life.

Chapter Fourteen

Perfectionist, Interrupted

"We only have one life on this earth in this body. ONE. You can be you, just as you are. Follow your own path as yourself and enjoy the ride. Live for all those people who didn't get to where you are. Live for the life that flows through us all."

Andie Mack

ANDIE MACK

ig: @buildingourbeautiful

Andie Mack

Andie is a full-time working mom of two amazing children, whom she raises with her British-born husband in Ontario, Canada. Her passions in life include travel, performing arts, health, family and friends. She considers herself a recovering perfectionist who is on a continuous journey to love herself and live free from superficial, unrealistic expectations. In 2017 she endured a debilitating concussion, which opened her up to self-healing in a way she never imagined. And then in 2018, she and her husband decided to get off the hamster wheel for a while and right-sized their home to free themselves up financially and live a more relaxed lifestyle. It was the best move they ever made, and they've never looked back.

Perfectionist, Interrupted

Many women call themselves perfectionists. In fact, we often lean-in to this moniker. Do *you* call yourself a perfectionist? Do you know people who do? Is it worn as a badge of honor? Have you noticed that we women casually throw it around? "I'm such a perfectionist." We give it credence as something we *should be* as mothers, daughters, wives, and workers.

Consider this common interview scenario:

Interviewer: "What is one thing you know you need to work on?"

Woman in interview, smugly knowing her words will work to her advantage: "Well, I would say that I'm a bit of a perfectionist—I won't rest until my work is to the highest standard."

Perfectionist. This word is extremely loaded. I invite you to consider what it means for you.

I needed a literal hit on the head to see how perfectionism was holding me hostage. I hope now to help other women escape its vice-grip. To live in this world inspired and free to be their truest selves.

Until my mid-thirties, when I was a mom of a four-year-old boy and seven-year-old girl, I branded myself a perfectionist, and perhaps was proud to do so. I accepted it as part of my personality—an immovable aspect of who I was. I confused perfectionism as synonymous with achievement, intelligence, and success. In retrospect, it was an enormous part of what held me back from living the life meant for me.

Perfection is the pinnacle, though, right? *Right*?? That's what I would tell myself. The problem is that it's a false summit, a mirage. There *is* no perfect. I've realized that by being perfectionistic and striving for that unattainable goal, we set ourselves up for disappointment and thus hold ourselves back from truly living. And since perfection is subjective, we can change the parameters of it and allow space to beat ourselves up for not attaining it.

Let's be clear: it is gratifying to work towards something we desire when it comes from a place of self-love. It's when we create a false image of what we should achieve and then criticize ourselves for not reaching it that we find ourselves in treacherous waters. *This is especially concerning for working mothers in today's society.* We're so bombarded with picture perfect images and information that we lose ourselves and our self-esteem trying to attain them.

Oh, how I used to beat myself up for not doing something *right* as both a mother and a worker. Anytime my kids watched TV, I felt like a terrible mother. At work, if I didn't get high praise and recognition for a job well done, I was a failure. It was a perfect storm that fueled my perfectionism. I grew miserable and anxious, but couldn't see the anxiety through my drive to achieve, to be perfect. I imagine many mothers can relate.

Take this scenario of a new mother struggling to breastfeed her baby:

A young mother has worked hard to breastfeed her baby, gone to the breastfeeding clinic and read the books. She hasn't used a soother or allowed the baby to have a bottle because she read it could cause "nipple confusion" and she didn't want that to interfere with her (quite unsuccessful) breastfeeding. Despite her desperate efforts, the milk doesn't come out fast enough for her baby, and baby can't seem to latch. Feedings are stressful—baby hungry, mom in pain. Baby wants to suckle, but her weary mom's nipples are cracked and bleeding. Mom pushes on without a soother or bottle, adamant that *her baby will **not** get nipple confusion.*

On a daily, sometimes hourly basis, mom cries in the shower and sobs before feedings. In her mind, she has to get this right. Because that's what mothers do, and she's telling herself somewhere in her consciousness that she's a failure if she doesn't. A perfect mother breast-feeds her baby, and it's beautiful, goddammit! So why can't she just do it?!

The people around her struggle to help and this mom is not pleasant to be around. One day, she's completely exhausted. Tears run down her face because the baby wants to suckle all day and she just can't take it anymore. Her mother and mother-in-law suggest trying a soother, to give her a break. Crestfallen, she gives in.

"Fine," she sighs, and starts sobbing.

She's reached her breaking point. To her chagrin, the baby gets the soother.

What happens next changes her.

The baby takes the soother like it's the most enjoyable thing she's ever had! Sucking away, she's as happy and content as a baby can be.

Relieved of her nipple torture, mom rests. Her body gets a break. A few days later she allows dad to feed baby formula from a bottle. Baby takes it, sleeps like, well, a baby, and the new little family gets some rest. Everyone feels human again. It's a rush of relief so great the mother wished she had come upon it sooner.

The struggle for this mom (who, as you may have guessed, was me) was real. Looking back on this ten years later, I can see the problem wasn't breastfeeding. It was a battle against perceived failure. I realized though that I knew in my heart what was right for my body and my baby. When I let go, I was able to see that we would be ok no matter what. I weaned my baby at six weeks and while it wasn't easy, I felt more confident in trusting my gut and going with the flow.

Motherhood was certainly an adjustment. It brought out the insecurities I could normally disguise at work. The breastfeeding experience taught me that I couldn't control this baby like I could manage a project at work—she had her own agenda.

It was a tremendous lesson in letting go.

In the end, the breastfeeding experience gave a blow to my armor of perfectionism. But it would take many more for it to crack. I was stubborn and kept building it back up, using it to protect myself against the unknown which I couldn't control. My pattern was to push for more at home and work, to achieve those impossible standards. Failure was my biggest fear.

THE RETURN TO WORK

My first return from maternity leave went relatively smoothly. For a perfectionist who loved to work and be rewarded for exemplary work, being off was difficult. Like many new moms, I felt alone, stuck, and useless. Perhaps I had a mild case of postpartum depression. So after about four months, I started working one day a week. I got a rush from the chance to do something productive again (as if raising another human isn't productive—hello!). I was still a new mother and an emotional wreck but I craved a sense of accomplishment outside of motherhood.

On one of those first days back, I was presenting my work back to some of the company's leaders in a virtual meeting. It didn't quite go as expected—the feedback felt direct and blunt and I recall feeling very hurt. It wasn't that anything had changed with my colleagues, but I wasn't used to the work environment. In my mind, I felt like I had just ventured into the light only to get blinded. It was a tough lesson in strad-dling the emotional aspects of being a working mom.

My second return from leave was when things really came off the rails. After my second was born, I had experienced significant physical issues. I took the full year off, and did manage to enjoy mother-hood once I had healed. When I returned to work though, things had changed. There were new leadership dynamics and my job description was different. I felt very out of place, like an alien in a foreign land. I muddled through, growing more anxious but pressuring myself to drive and deliver, so that I could prove my worth.

GETTING AHEAD

When my kids were four and one, I decided to change jobs and companies. I was excited about the challenge. But man oh man! Making this change with two young kids was more difficult than I could have imagined. The neverending illness, the daycare drama, and the pres-sure to show off to people who did not know my abilities? It called my perfectionist to attention in a big way.

You want me to prove that we can do it all,
with a cherry on top? You got it, boss!

At this job I got exceptional ratings, promotions, and accolades. I drove to achieve and felt accomplished but something was wrong. I was constantly stressed. I cried all the time. And it only got worse. The harder things felt, the harder I pushed. I wanted the next promotion. My husband and I started to dream of more: a bigger house, more money, more renovations, more travel, another car... more more *more*. And my perfectionist was there to make it all happen.

Perfectionism is like the hitman, who with a
snap of a finger can, and will, get it done.

THE MOMENT IT ALL CHANGED

After several years, I had reached a breaking point. I had thought a few times about therapy, about going back to the antidepressant that helped me in my twenties. For some reason though—pride, denial, shame—I didn't take action. So, one day, the universe took action for me.

If I wasn't sure about universal energy before, I am now. It is powerful beyond measure.

I recall the moment vividly. I came home from work, in a pleasant mood (for once) to learn that my son had an issue with a classmate at school. So, in the middle of our newly renovated kitchen, I squatted down to get on eye level with him and asked him what happened. We chatted about it for a moment, then, as four-year-olds do, he abruptly jumped up in the middle of our conversation. As he jumped, his forehead hit my forehead squarely in the middle with a force so great it knocked me back in my squatting position. As I flew backwards, the back of my head smacked directly into the cornered edge of the new quartz countertop. It was like a car accident, when the head hits the steering wheel then the cushioned headrest. Except this was my son's hard skull and a stone counter.

It literally knocked the wind out of me.

I didn't pass out, but I was shaken, and something in me immediately changed. At that moment, I had a primal awareness that I was not the same. The pain in my head was indescribable. After I recovered from the initial shock, I was emotionless. Apathetic. It was as though *I* was gone.

Unsurprisingly, I had a concussion and whiplash (my son was fine, thankfully). The experience of recovery would take me months—even years. I couldn't work—I could barely hold a conversation without sweating profusely and getting so exhausted I couldn't speak anymore. I couldn't hold my head up, concentrate, or do any one activity for over ten minutes. Emotionally, it felt like the lights had been turned off.

When I started experiencing emotion again, I was all over the place. I felt devastated, frightened and completely out of control. I was terrified I would never be the same again. Little did I know that's exactly what I needed.

I spent the next several months working on myself. For the first time in my life, I had to put myself first; I literally did not have the capacity for anything else. All remaining energy I had went towards my children. There was nothing else left.

I saw eight different specialists, simultaneously, and worked hard to get the neurons in my brain to function again. I had intense anxiety

(I realize now it was the untreated anxiety I had felt before, compounded by the concussion). I sought alternative treatments like acupuncture, Chinese medicine, and psychotherapy to manage it. I also finally spoke to my doctor about getting back on the low-dose prescription treatment that had worked for me before. I began to gain some balance and perspective.

I finally saw clearly the devastating impact
perfectionism had on my life.

Through the recovery experience, I reclaimed my true self and got to know myself better. I realized that the good side of the perfectionism coin was my resourcefulness, which is a wonderful tool when not clouded by its evil twin. It was often my resourcefulness that got me through difficult situations and helped me succeed at work. The perfectionism got in the way.

In recovery, I felt deep gratitude for the little things, like being able to make a batch of muffins or multiplying seven by seven without a calculator. I was incredibly appreciative of my support system—health providers, good friends, family, my husband. Everyone respected my space and offered invaluable encouragement and support.

I was fortunate that my disability leave allowed me five months off work completely, plus another five in a gradual return. But when I finally returned to work full time, things were different. Work was different. I had changed.

When I felt compelled to push again, I didn't. I physically couldn't. My body was a reminder to put myself and my health first. For that, I am eternally grateful.

Life evolved greatly following this experience
and my personal growth accelerated.

This lesson has been the most profound of my life. I have come to understand and respect my own boundaries and truths. I am learning to be led by love and by the most important things in my life—my relationships and my self-compassion. I still want to work hard, and achieve great things, but I'm taking a new path, one that feels aligned with my values and my true self.

To this day, I still have physical symptoms and I don't know if they'll ever go away. I believe they are a reminder to listen to myself until I no longer need the lesson.

After my recovery, we took a much-needed vacation. It was during our time away that my husband and I realized we needed less, not more. We then decided to sell our house and relocate our family to a home with a smaller price tag and much less maintenance—we called it *right-sizing*. We have never once regretted the decision.

The equity from our old house enabled me to leave the corporate life for a while and focus on my family and my health. I was able to embark on a project with my husband, a condo flip, which ended up being an emotional boon for our relationship. It taught us how to work together, and be there for one another. I dabbled in entrepreneurship and engaged with a whole new community that I didn't know existed. It has had a huge influence on my personal growth.

By letting go of the unnecessary things, we became closer as a couple and a family.

Perhaps you've gone through your own traumatic experience. Or perhaps you're struggling like I was. Whatever your situation, make peace with yourself. Being a working mom is difficult, and so often we get clouded by ego and perfectionism. We get caught up in the *should* and dim our own light.

I invite you to explore your truth. If you're in resistance, constantly feel overextended, or if you're suffering, you are not alone. Learn to really listen to yourself without judgement. Get help if you need it. Finally, invite in unconditional self-love and compassion. It is the key to unlock a more fulfilled and satisfied life.

Chapter Fifteen

Positive Mindset is Essential

"We can determine to be happy and look on the bright side, expecting and believing good things will happen."

Nanci Lozano

NANCI LOZANO

www.nancilozano.com
ig: @nancilozano | fb: @nancilozano

Nanci Lozano

Nanci Lozano is an inspiration; she is an entrepreneur, warrior, and life-style trainer. At sixty years young she is full of energy and ideas to help people lose weight and be in the best shape of their life. She is a knowledgeable and curious single mother of five (and great-grandmother) who loves life, takes on challenges, and fights hard for herself and those she loves. Dedicated to bodybuilding, she has placed first internationally and nationally among women twenty to thirty years younger than her. Nanci is currently working on obtaining her pro card as a Figure Competitor. She was published in *Iron Magazine* in Japan as first place winner in the open division. She mastered getting her power back: mind, body, and soul.

Born and raised in Sacramento, California, Nanci was an honorable student, cheerleader, track team member, and first runner-up for student Queen. After her father retired they moved to a poor neighborhood, where her and her father cared for her sick mother. Nanci remained focused on the positive and eventually pursued studies in criminal justice and political science that led her to law school. She had a fantastic career with the Attorney General's Office, Department of Justice for thirty-five years. After retiring at the age of fifty-three she realized she was not ready to stop and continued with a private law firm.

Now an author, she hopes to motivate others to pursue happiness, no matter what age. She is an open book and you can absolutely reach out to train with her.

Positive Mindset is Essential

My father taught me at a very young age to work hard, to mind my own business, to be respectful, and good things will happen. My mother was outspoken and a very strong, determined woman. She expected me to be a nurse and work in a hospital like her. However, life doesn't always turn out the way other people expect of you or sometimes even the way you expect it. In fact, I had no idea I would be married to the first guy I kissed at the young age of sixteen, and have three sons and divorced by the time I was eighteen years old. I was the first and only person in my family to get a divorce and I am the youngest. During that time many people looked down on me for being so young as a single parent raising boys. I remember my own mother telling me that "I would never amount to anything and she was ashamed of me for getting a divorce." Instead of feeling sorry for myself, I used her harsh comment as my aggression and strength to do something positive with my life.

During that time as a single parent I felt overwhelmed, worried, anxious, and stressed out, but I had to keep going for my sons. I didn't have a minute to rest. I would run three miles at the park and lift weights at the gym because it made me feel good and gave me the mental and emotional strength to keep going. With all the sports practices my sons had, working full time, and going to school full time, I was busy. I would read my college books on the bleacher while my sons were practicing. Now that I look back at my life, I realize how far I have come along. I crossed paths with certain people for life or seasons, under God's reasons, to learn more about myself and how I could integrate lessons with life skills. Life lessons taught me to be an independent, stronger, intelligent woman and showed me how to better myself and serve those around me. God's plan was amazing.

In high school I was an honor roll student, a cheerleader, a song leader, first runner-up for homecoming queen, on the track team, and played volleyball and tennis. I tried to hide my pregnancy, but at seven months pregnant I was showing and had to leave public school and attend a continuation school. I felt humiliated because I was a popular honor roll student and now I had to attend a school with some hard knock kids. I eventually took my GED in June at the same time my previous classmates were graduating from high school.

In July, I got my first job with the Attorney General's Office, Department of Justice at eighteen years old, working in the mailroom and started community college to further my career. Many of the attorneys guided me in college. I worked myself up the ranks at DOJ and then went to California State University of Los Angeles, graduated after seven years, and then later went on to law school. At the young age of fifty-three, I retired with the DOJ with thirty-five years of service and a full pension.

I read my favorite scripture Jeremiah 29:11 every single day and at my graduation ceremony I wore a sash with the scripture engraved:

"For I know the plans I have for you, declares the Lord,
Plans to prosper you and not to harm you,
Plans to give you hope and a future."

I remember reading this scripture over and over every single day to give me hope and strength to provide for my sons. I used to wonder why life is so hard. Why do I always run out of money? Why do I feel alone and frustrated and exhausted? I was a young shy girl trying to figure out life raising kids alone. We didn't have cell phones, computers, or any of the technology that we have today. Life was much harder because their father was never around to help me. He was suffering from an alcohol and drug addiction. But I had my sons to keep me going. When I look back at all the obstacles we went through in life and all the accomplishments, there's nothing more joyful in my heart than to see the brotherly love among all my sons today. I raised them to be there for each other no matter what and that family always comes first. Today my sons instill the same belief with their children and all of my grandchildren are very close.

Every month I used my sick leave and then
used vacation to cover all the sick days
because when one son got sick they would all
get sick.

Even though times were hard, I always had a curious mind, and I would read. I would read motivational books and self-help books to be a better person. I would have my kids read books or do their homework while I studied. On weekends when they didn't have homework I would put wrestling figures on the table and give each one of them a drawing sketch pad to practice drawing. Today they are all good artists.

CHOOSE TO BE A GREAT ROLE MODEL WITH A POSITIVE MENTALITY

Our children are always watching us. We have to be positive role models and provide a safe, loving, healthy environment for them. As much as we love them and want to be that "cool parent," we must encourage them to have respect and be cordial. If we don't teach our kids to be respectful, they will be disrespectful and walk all over us, and not take us seriously. We don't want to raise spoiled kids. We want our kids to turn out with qualities like compassion, good morals, and kindness. If we spoil children and give them everything they want, our children will grow up overly pampered, overly indulged, under disciplined, and not compassionate. In fact, many parents aren't aware that they are spoiling their kids. Here are some signs to watch for:

1. *Do they play well with others?*
2. *Do they drive people away?*
3. *Do they have tantrums?*
4. *Are they helpful?*
5. *Do they say "thank you"?*
6. *Do they say "I need" instead of "May I please have"?*

While children can certainly express excitement about how badly they want something, they should learn to make requests rather than demands. If you have teenage kids be sure to get involved with the school, volunteer, and check their backpacks. Kids do not have a privacy right; you have a right to know what your kid is doing and with whom they are socializing. If you give your child too much freedom to hangout and go wherever he or she pleases, you will have problems. Keep them in sports or something they are passionate about. Of course they're going to tell you, "Mom, I don't want to do that," but a child does not know what he or she needs. I used to sign my youngest son Joseph up for sports and he would get upset with me and say, "No, I don't want to play baseball, I hate it," but he never played before. Regardless of what he said, I would sign him up, pick him up, and take him to practice and study for college classes while sitting in the bleachers. It went on like this for years. As he got older and during the summer I would sign him up for professional sports camps at Pepperdine University and many other universities so he could learn skills taught by the professionals.

When he was in the second grade, I noticed he was talented at drawing. His second grade teacher, Mrs. Feldman, told me about an art school and that I should put him in art lessons. I got a second job and stopped going to school for a quarter to put him in private art classes. He learned the fundamentals of drawing, painting, and color theory. He did excellent in art school and it came naturally to him. This was his gift. Throughout the years in school he advanced in art and had his work displayed at the museum, and he was accepted to San Francisco State University, living with all his friends he knew since the sixth grade.

One day he called me and said, "Mama please sit down, I have to tell you something." I did, and I listened. He told me to trust him, he knew what he was doing, and that he dropped out of college. Today he is a music producer, and produces music for music artists and travels around the world meeting people on his gigs. My point is: putting him in sports taught him to be a team player. Putting him in a private art school was worth it even though I had to work two jobs because it advanced his artistic talent. Everyone loves him because he communicates well. People recognize his outstanding work ethics and his great talent and artistry of music.

As a child you love your parents no matter what. My parents helped me a lot with my sons. My sons loved going over to their grandparents' house. It was fun watching them play with all their cousins and enjoy all the birthday parties and holiday gatherings. But things were not always stable with my mother because she was really sick. She was diabetic, epileptic, and had seizure attacks often. She wouldn't follow her doctor's orders and eventually she abused prescribed medications, and she died at a young age.

I couldn't bring any of my friends over because I was afraid for them to see her messed up on pills or laid out in bed in the middle of the day. She was sick most of my life as far back as I could remember, since I was five years old. This was hard for me as a child because I did not understand why she looked high and depressed some days and other days she was happy. I couldn't comprehend why or how she could stay up all night making noise and I couldn't sleep. The ambulance would come over to our house every month because she was having seizure attacks. I would scream and cry thinking she was going to die. I remember being embarrassed at school because the kids would crowd around me and ask if my mother died.

As an adult, I wanted to be a good example for my kids and never wanted to be like my mother. I strived to be like my father and live a young, happy, and healthy life. My father is now ninety eight years old and still living strong and happy.

My father is a kind, strong gentleman, who was in the army and served two wars. He's always been a positive role model and made an honest career as a foreman providing for seven kids. We had everything and never suffered from not having enough. He was a boy scout leader and would take all the kids hiking, camping, and taught survival techniques. I still have great memories from those amazing trips.

As a kid I remember waking up at 6:00 a.m. watching my father do exercises with Jack LaLanne on television. I would see him doing push-ups and working out. Then he would serve me cream of wheat. I knew at a young age I wanted to do good deeds, and be happy and healthy like my father. I had so much respect for him and everyone in the neighborhood knew my father and had respect for him. He would go out of his way to help people. Two times I witnessed him saving people. Our neighbor's house caught on fire and he ran into the house to save the family. Another time, the levee broke, and a woman was stranded in a flood with her car and a child. My father put me on his car rooftop and told me to stay on top, don't move, and that he was going to help the woman and child—he would come right back for me. I was five years old, and I did exactly as he said and watched him put the woman and child on a big tire with a rope and pulled them onto dry land. Then we gave them a ride home.

I joined my first gym, the Jack LaLanne Health Club, when I was eighteen years old. Jack LaLanne was known as the Godfather of fitness, and the First Fitness Superhero. I had no idea what I was doing. I would buy *Muscle & Fitness* magazines and read them and learn. I would walk into the men's weight room and the men would stare me down like: what are you doing in here. Back then women were frowned on if they lifted weights in the men's weight room. I would raise my head and walk in like I had confidence and act like I knew what I was doing. After a while, I did know what I was doing, and I loved going to the gym every single day.

STAY IN THE MOMENT

Having a positive mindset is essential even if you're living in a dysfunctional environment. Every day we get to choose our attitudes. We can be determined to be happy and look on the bright side expecting good things to happen and believing we will accomplish our dreams, or we could choose to be negative by focusing on our problems, dwelling on the past, or what didn't work out.

I could have focused on my past and been discouraged, but I never look back unless it's a good memory. Life will go so much better if you decide to be a positive person. When you wake up in the morning, choose to be happy.

Positive Mindset is Essential

Think about all the good things you have and how grateful you are for your life.

If you don't choose to be happy in the morning when you first wake up, then more than likely you will default into a negative mindset thinking negative thoughts, such as: *I don't feel like going to the gym. I don't feel good. I don't want to go to work. My friend posted something on Instagram that hurt my feelings.*

It's not the circumstances that make you negative, it's your negative thinking about those circumstances.

Section Four

Survival Guide: Mom-Hacks 101

FEATURING:

Charleyne Oulton
Laura Morris
Stephanie Card
Erin Montgomery
Sharlene Rochard

Chapter Sixteen

Real Advice From a Real Busy Mom

"Work and home life balance. Can it really exist?"

Charleyne Oulton

CHARLEYNE OULTON

www.coachcharleybrown.com
ig: @coachcharleybrown | goodreads: Charleyne Oulton
Portraiture by: Katie Jean Photography, Mill Bay, British Columbia

Charleyne Oulton

Charleyne Oulton, #coachcharleybrown, lives on Vancouver Island in British Columbia and is an 4x Amazon bestselling and 4x award-winning author, a reserve member of the Canadian Armed Forces, a mother of three teenagers, and is determined to maintain a life filled with health and harmony for herself and for her family whilst juggling a very demanding career.

Real Advice From a Real Busy Mom

To be frank, I do not get enough sleep. I am lousy at staying asleep. I know some people who can sleep sitting up, catch up on zzz's at a dental appointment, and practically fall asleep in minutes—and yet I toss and turn all night long. I can never seem to quiet my mind and no matter how hard I try, I cannot stop listening for the kids. My children are twelve, thirteen, and fifteen years old; they are not babies! Yet, when they sneeze, or get up to go to the washroom at night or come down the stairs to grab some water, it wakes me up instantly! I cannot seem to turn off my mom radar. I have tried sleep meditations, sound machines, even melatonin, and I still cannot sleep more than five hours per night on average. So when my alarm goes off in the morning at 5:15 a.m., I am cranky, and not just a little cranky, I am Cruella De Vil cranky.

I am not a morning person, but I have learned how to have a successful morning and get everyone out the door on time in less than one hour! It comes down to organization and streamlining my family routine. I plan for the morning the night before. We pack lunches, go over the next day's sports, work, school calendar, and sometimes we even pack the truck the night before. I've taught my kids to pick out their clothing and pack their backpacks before they go to bed. My husband-to-be and I double-check that the coffee pot has been set, and that we have our travel and coffee mugs ready to go; and before I crawl into bed, I even make sure the dogs and cats have fresh kibble and water, so they can eat breakfast in the morning without me having to remember to feed them! By doing all of this, I have created a morning routine that allows me to focus on my family rather than my to-do list. Being a working mom, my time with my family is very limited. I am sure this is the same for all working parents, and creating a rhythm and successful work-home life balance proves to be a juggling act.

Nobody hustles harder than a mother juggling children and a career. Nobody!

Having a successful career and raising children is tough for so many reasons. I miss my children when I am at work. I think of them all day. Seriously. Even though my children are no longer little, I miss talking to them, I wonder if they are having a good day at school and with their friends. It pains me when I cannot attend a hockey or lacrosse practice, or game. Or when I have no choice but to miss Girl Guides or Cadet adventures. I try my absolute best, but it has proven impossible to be in two places at once. Darn!

Being a reserve member in the Canadian Armed Forces I do not have a typical nine to five work schedule, I have a "from when I open my eyes to when I close my eyes" schedule. That is a sacrifice I make for my family and for our country. Sometimes I am away for weeks on end. Sometimes longer. It is easy to get overwhelmed with everything, which is why it is so vital for my sanity to find and maintain work-life harmony that includes time to be unplugged and present with my family, time alone with my spouse, time outside or playing with my pets, even time for exercise. I schedule everything and I write everything down in my calendar, which thanks to my smartphone, I can sync with my children, spouse, and even my mom (who is our personal dog daycare, taxi driver, board game player, and sometimes meal cooker). I even have to set alarms to remind myself to drink water. Truly. Or I find myself very thirsty at the end of the day.

I have learned the hard way that it is OKAY and necessary for me to set boundaries, and that it is okay to politely say "NO" to certain things that are asked of me. I was a stay-at-home mom for the first twelve years of parenting. My priority was my children's health and happiness. My only juggle was their activities and schedules, and I was fortunate enough to work from home, which allowed me to be present for their every need and want. I was on the PTA board, I was always available for birthday parties, playdates, and even to watch other moms' children. But, things changed when I found myself going through a divorce and beginning to work outside of our family home for the first time in my adult and parenting life. I had to get comfortable with saying NO. "No, I cannot volunteer for the upcoming field trip, or in the classroom," and "I cannot help you make valentine's cards for three classes," or "deliver food for hot lunch day. Sorry! No!" I could no longer have unexpected playdates or watch a child who has to miss school because they are sick, while I cannot even attend my own children's extracurricular activities.

BUT, I am more present and available for my children when I am with them than I ever was being a stay-at-home mom. Isn't that ironic? So before I agree to a commitment that is asked of me, I stop, I ask myself *is this something you want to do?* I check my calendar and my availability. I consider what else I could be doing during that time and then I make an informed decision, that way I do not wind up feeling mommy guilt.

Charleyne Oulton

I think neglecting ourselves and mommy guilt are two of the biggest struggles moms in our culture deal with today.

Can I be honest? All of the career moms I am friends with admit to suffering mom guilt at some point during their career. I struggle with this regularly. I'm sometimes away from my children for weeks on end, whether that's because of work or because of shared custody. Either way, I miss birthdays, school events, and sometimes am not available to personally pick up my sick child from school. And it sucks.

Whether you're a working mom, a single mom, or a stay at home mom, it just seems like our to-do lists are never done, always growing. If I am home, I am usually cleaning, cooking, meal prepping, or doing laundry. Although these chores are constant and important, I have learned it is even more crucial to spend as much time with my kids as possible. Therefore in our household, I encourage and include my children in housework, scheduling, and cooking. Sometimes this time together while folding socks, cooking a meal, or walking our dogs is the only time I have available to be with them on that day. This might seem like a chore to them, but to me it is time I cherish. So I turn on the music and make it fun.

Our children are growing up every single second of every single day. Time with our children is precious, it is also time that is not promised, or guaranteed, so I strongly encourage you to carve out time for them every chance possible. There are only 24 hours in a day, only 365 days in a year. There is no pause button in life. I have learned to get better at managing my time and organizing our life to maximize the slight amount of time that I have available to be with my family. I have learned to delegate; whether it be splurging and hiring a maid occasionally, so I can take the kids on a long hike; or dropping the dogs off at dog daycare, so we can do something special that is hard to do with two dogs! Sometimes it's as easy as getting things done in advance to free up a day or an afternoon. I have learned how to make mundane daily taskings quicker and easier. We keep a very organized house so clean up is quick. Everyone knows where everything goes. Even our dogs have a basket for their toys! We try hard to never let the house get out of control, and I buy cleaning products safe to use for our whole family; that are multipurpose so we can use one spray of cleaner throughout the house.

We have introduced several small changes that continually free up more time for us to be together.

I geographically limit my children's activities, playdates, and plans to one central area. As much as possible. Of course this is not always reasonable, but eighty-five percent of the time my childrens' sports, jobs, and extracurricular activities are all in the same area of town. This means I am not driving back and forth and all over the place. This is a huge time saver for me. It also means my kids can walk from their school to where they need to be if I am working late or unavailable. I have taught my children to use public transport. Something I thought I would never allow them to do. It caused a lot of anxiety for me, at first, but it has taught my children responsibility, to work together, to navigate, and has given them the ability to get home without me.

I have even taught my children how to grocery shop by themselves. It started with just one item and now they are all able to go through the fridge and pantry, make a list, get to the grocery store, choose and buy groceries. What an incredible life skill. I love to utilize grocery delivery services whenever possible. Having the ability to have your groceries delivered has been a blessing when I choose to spend my time with my children rather than at the grocery store. Sometimes I really am grateful for this technology filled era we live in. Depending on where you live, there are probably a few different grocery delivery or shopping services, and I encourage you to try these programs.

Since becoming a working mom, I don't think I've ever felt so perpetually short on time—I can attest that there are seemingly never enough hours in the day. To help us stay on time I continually confuse my spouse by saving timings in our phone calendars WRONG. For example: If Cadets end at 9:00 p.m., I have it saved in our phones, with a reminder that Cadets end at 8:30 p.m! If Hockey Academy starts at 7:30 a.m., the alarm goes off notifying us it starts at 7:00 a.m. This drives my family absolutely bonkers, BUT it ensures that we always arrive on time, and it works for me.

Let go of the mom-guilt mama, give yourself grace.

You are not a bad mom for leaving your children when you go to work or happen to manage to carve out time for yourself. Moms have been leaving their children for centuries—nursemaids, wet nurses, nannies, and boarding schools are all found in history. And while the concept of mom guilt isn't necessarily new, it is vastly intensified in today's world as we are more connected than ever before. Unfortunately, working mom guilt isn't something you can just snap out of on a whim. I can tell you not to feel guilty until I'm blue in the face, that you are doing a great job as a mother, and that your children will turn out perfect. All of these are true. You've got to believe these things for yourself. Learn how to cope and reach that level of understanding. Most importantly, remember to be patient and kind to yourself.

I offer myself grace and acceptance for being imperfect because I know perfectionism is impossible in this chapter of life. So what if I did not shave my legs today, or we have breakfast for dinner tonight. It's more than okay to be scruffy and eat eggs for dinner. I value conversation and community over tidiness. I'd rather spend time with my child than pretend to be Instagram perfect all of the time. My children love me regardless of my nails being painted, and eyebrows being on point. I don't have to pretend to be the supermom who doesn't exist. My home is welcoming, our authenticity shines, even if my floors do not. My children are proud of me. They have watched me work hard. They have watched me grow. They know I do the best I can, both at home and at work, and I am full of gratitude for their unwavering love, encouragement, and support.

If I can achieve both parenting and career success, then it is possible for you as well!

Pat yourself on your back, you are probably your worst critic.

Much Love,

Charleyne

Chapter Seventeen

Say No and Let Go

"Thankfully, having my first child rocked my world in so many ways, and I may have never learned the important skill of saying 'no' if he hadn't been born."

Laura Morris

LAURA MORRIS

ig: @mslauramorris | fb: Laura Morris

Laura Morris

Laura is a mom to three energetic, feral boys, stepmom to three more, wife, school administration student, wellness coach, and full-time educator. Life can get busy and she admittedly has spent a significant amount of time lost in the madness. Lucky for Laura, after her sons were born she learned a valuable lesson: caring for herself permitted her to care for everyone else more effectively. In Laura's case, this comes in several forms: exercise, balanced nutrition, curling up with a book and some coffee (or let's be real . . . a stiff drink), cooking and dancing in the kitchen, connecting with other women, and writing.

Sharing her story and struggles is a form of therapy, and not only benefits Laura, but other women who battle their own demons. Becoming more comfortable with being real has given her more freedom and confidence than she has ever felt before, and she refuses to go back into hiding.

One of Laura's life's passions is to connect with other women and encourage them to spend the time getting to know themselves—and getting to love themselves—whatever stage of life they are in. As moms, allowing ourselves the grace we give to others can be a struggle, but one of the best ways to learn a new skill is to surround yourself with others working toward the same.

Laura's husband and their combined five (soon to be six) kids, live in central New York.

Say No and Let Go

I knew I was losing it when I started making up songs to the sound of my breast pump working away. The mechanical in-out was so unlike the soft sighs and chuckles of my nursing newborn that it was comical, but probably not as comical as the sight of me sitting in the strange meeting room, work blouse unbuttoned, nursing bra shoved aside, and me balancing one foot on the round table, so I could hold both flanges on my breasts with one hand while precariously using my knee as another support. Why put my healing-from-childbirth body through such acrobatics you ask? So I could have one hand free to scroll my phone for pictures and videos, so I could see my baby. Strangely enough, I found it helped ever so slightly with milk production while I spent my days away from him at work.

The act of lugging my pump with me to work (which took me to various locations all around the state), making sure my ice packs were frozen when I left the house at 5:00 a.m., having enough milk storage bags, cleaning supplies, sanitizing steamer bags for the pump parts (in case I was lucky enough to have a microwave I could use), extra batteries, nursing pads for the inevitable leaking that would take place at some point during the day, and anything else I might need while I was away, had become a part of my already overwhelming *getting out the door* routine. Not only was getting out the door stressful, but walking back in the door had quickly become another source for my feelings of inadequacy.

Naively I thought I would continue to be capable of the tasks I handled with ease before my son was born. Not that caring for our home before we added a baby was easy; I stepped into a marriage with a man who had three beautiful kids from his first marriage who were still young and involved in multiple sports and activities. We shared fifty percent custody with their mom with exchanges between houses happening several times a week, folding in two dogs and a cat, along with our decent-sized home with several acres, chickens, and enough laundry, cooking, and cleaning to put the famously large Kardashian family to shame (and without the hired help). Add in one tiny, premature five pound newborn with acid reflux who needed to be held twenty-four, seven and suddenly I couldn't function at all.

Now, much of this was my doing. I stepped into the relationship with the mind to **do it all**. Cook and clean for everyone daily? Yep! Grocery shop? You got it! Pay the bills? On it. Run kids to sports practice or friends' houses? Of course! Take care of the animals? I LOVE that stuff.

Dentist and doctor appointments? Sure! All while working a full-time job and teaching as an adjunct professor on the side. I'm unsure what piece was missing within myself at that time in my life that made me feel the appropriate way to fill that space was to seek approval through *doing*. Like many women, I prided myself on the ability to handle multiple things at once and I was efficient at it. My love language[1] is acts of service, so naturally *doing* is how I show my family I love them. It had never occurred to me that the very thing that expressed my love could eventually drag me crashing and burning into severe anxiety attacks and depression.

> *Thankfully, having my first child rocked my world in so many ways, and I may have never learned the important skill of saying 'no' if he hadn't been born.*

The funny thing is, I was still doing a decent job of juggling it all until my twelve-week maternity leave ended and I had to go back to work to help keep our household finances in the black. It was then, when my world changed yet again, that I realized I would have to put some things down and allow my family to pick up the slack, in order to save myself. And that's exactly what it was: an act of self-love and saving myself from impending mental and emotional disaster. That may sound like an overkill description, but for me, that is exactly what was happening.

I come from a long line of women who seem to effortlessly manage and orchestrate households without breaking a sweat. They make it seem so easy that I never fully understood the heavy price of such management until I was the matriarch of my nest. My grandmother had eight siblings growing up and naturally was expected to pull her own weight with the chores, and this work ethic ebbed into her adult life. My mother deserves to be canonized as an official saint due to the selflessness she demonstrated for my father, brother, and me. When I think about what life must have been like for her when we were young, I typically pick up my phone to text her and say how much I appreciate her. She worked full time, came home and finished the chores with my father (a dairy farmer), and then took responsibility for all the cooking, cleaning, and childcare necessary that evening. I never remember hearing her com-

1   Gary Chapman, "The 5 Love Languages," Moody Bible Institute (website), last modified June 6, 2007, https://www.5lovelanguages.com/book/the-5-love-languages/.

plain. I can only recollect one instance of her losing her cool and crying because her darling daughter (yes, that's me) refused to get dressed when we were already late getting out the door. As an adult, I realize a lot had to take place behind the scenes to make sure we were all taken care of, but I internalized the messaging I had received as a young girl, that it is up to me to coordinate and execute it all. And have heels on while I do it.

Once I realized that continuing at this breakneck pace was not only impossible, but irresponsible of me, you would think cutting back would be an easy next step. It wasn't. The idea itself is simple. Actually executing it is a big change not only for me, but my family. They were all used to my typical level of operation that my steps back seemed almost like a betrayal. What had they done to cause this change? Did I not love them anymore? How are we supposed to (insert job I typically did) without you? I am not saying they were not capable, over time they have all picked up the slack, and we have adjusted, but the initial shock felt similar to being shoved into a pool of icy water without warning. Or perhaps those feelings were all in my head and they were just waiting for the opportunity to solidify our unity as a family by more equally pitching in. I have to be open to the idea that the helplessness I placed on them is of my doing. If you're anything like me, this is a very real possibility.

I never considered myself a type A personality (or even having many of those qualities, honestly), until I had to allow other people to complete the tasks I had to rescind. One of the hardest lessons I continue to learn five years after the birth of my first son is this: *just because someone is doing something differently than I do, does not mean it is wrong or inferior.*

This process has taught me about myself. Apparently there *is* a *right* way to make a bed or place things in the refrigerator in my mind. Allowing my step children to pack their own lunches for school and risk (gasp!) them not putting both a serving of fruit *and* veggies in with their sandwich made my skin crawl. When I stopped checking backpacks for permission forms or other school communication, we missed a few deadlines, but the kids quickly learned to pull out anything important for their dad and I to check. My husband can, in fact, make his own doctor and dentist appointments, prescription refills, and balance his checkbook. The world will not end if I don't do it.

When I decided to make these changes, I took action immediately. To be honest, I didn't even have a formal conversation with my husband or stepchildren about how I was feeling or why I needed to make these changes. That was my mistake. If I had the opportunity for a do-over, I would be sure to include my family in my decision-making process:

1. Reflect on how you are feeling. Write it down, put it in a voice note on your phone.

2. Make a list of the tasks that seem to stress you out the most. It can be a small one, or a big one. It doesn't matter.

3. Sit down with your family, without phones or tablets. Get face-to-face and get real. Let them see and feel your stress and anxiety. Even if your children are young, showing emotion openly is a beautiful way to teach them it's okay to cry. It's okay to need help.

4. Share the list of tasks that are causing you stress. Brainstorm how you can work as a family to share the load.

5. Choose one or two changes to make at one time. Please, for the love of all that is holy, don't make a thousand changes at once. Start small, build momentum. The changes are more likely to stick that way.

6. Revisit with your partner and update each other on how things are going. Does anything need tweaking? What else from the list can we cross off for you, mama?

7. Is there anything we can outsource? Maybe grocery delivery is an option in your area. Or have someone come to your home once or twice a month to clean? Can you trade off child care with a friend every so often for some downtime?

This list is not exhaustive. In no way is it the proverbial keys to the kingdom. These are merely some suggestions that work for my family. Honestly, I'm still working on these things myself. I'll likely never be done or perfect at it, but I'll keep at it. That's all we can do, mamas.

Once things on the home-front had fallen into more of a *new normal*, I felt more mentally and emotionally prepared to catch up in my professional life, and ensure I was providing excellent services to the educators I was supporting as a behavior specialist. In this position, it was my responsibility to digest all the education law and direction coming from our state capital, and develop professional development and coaching sessions for school administrators and educators in my region. I felt the heaviness of the responsibility I was charged with towards these men and women, and for the students they served daily.

I take this important work seriously. I felt a bit of guilt for taking the full twelve-week unpaid maternity leave allowed by my workplace, our family couldn't financially swing me not returning to work. However, I would be bold-faced lying if I said I was physically or emotionally ready to return to work full time, leave my son at home, and immediately *knock it out of the park* at work. He was barely three months old, and had been born unexpectedly three weeks early. I was still nursing (which meant I had to pump several times throughout the workday to maintain my supply). He was *far* from sleeping through the night. As a matter of fact, he would only sleep on my chest in a reclining rocking chair until he was about a year old. Needless to say, my sleep wasn't excellent, either.

Sound familiar, mamas?

I do not see how anybody in their right mind could expect any person to perform at their best under those circumstances. I also believe it necessary to vocalize that my workplace at this time was wonderful and understanding of me as a new mom returning to my schedule. I know not every parent has this. I count myself lucky. Despite this, I found myself having to make decisions to save my sanity and well-being, but this time it was in the workplace.

Saying "no" at work is much more complicated than it is at home.

It's not like you can say no to the boss when they ask last-minute tasks of you, or if you get a phone call requesting a last-minute meeting. However, it is possible to say no to *some* things, and in turn, say yes to yourself. You may not necessarily be the most popular in the office for a while if you do these things, but if you're barely sleeping at night and have a needy child and family at home, you might feel like I did, and not give a crap. Balancing your goals at work with your current workload is a great way to ensure you're within your lane professionally in this process. The things I found helpful (if not necessary) to eliminate include:

1. Things that do not directly connect or contribute to your professional goals or responsibilities.

2. Writing references or recommendations for people that you don't one-hundred percent support.

3. Responding to emails, calls, or texts twenty-four hours a day. This is a big one. Shut down that work email after the day is done and do not pick it back up until it's time. Trust me on this one.

4. Contributing (financially or your time) to work parties, celebrations, etc. for individuals you are not very close to.

5. Extra work when you have already taken on more than your share.

*Remember, always be respectful when using the word **"no,"** and also remember that **"no"** is a complete sentence.*

Lucky for us, mamas, the exhaustion will fade. The babies will grow up and will not need to nurse every few hours. Even the breast pump and its hidden songs will retire and begin gathering dust in some random closet in your home. One day, you'll get a full night of sleep. The laundry will be done, the dishwasher emptied, and you may even have time for a bath and some quiet. The work you do in *and* out of the home is important, but not your only responsibility. Ensuring you're taking care of yourself in each place is necessary. You are equally mom and professional. You are fully both, and fully kicking ass in each role.

Chapter Eighteen

It's Okay to Be Selfish, Mama

*"Making yourself a priority isn't selfish,
it's smart!"*

Stephanie Card

STEPHANIE CARD

ig: @mom_with_goals | @bria_co_cookies_cakes
fb: @stephanie.tobias.7 | li: Stephanie Card
Goodreads: www.goodreads.com/user/show
/112259120-stephanie-card

Stephanie Card

Stephanie Card has always been one to strive for success and never quit or back down. Stephanie has always had an interest in law enforcement; thus leading her to study Law and Security Administration. Stephanie has been in the field of Corrections for the past ten years, which allows her to deal with people from all walks of life. Working in this environment led to a lot of negative thoughts, emotions, and struggles. Stephanie is also a proud social marketer who owns a global online health and wellness business. She has learned much about the importance of personal growth and development, and maintaining a positive outlook on life. Stephanie married her husband in 2015, and they welcomed their first child in 2016. Stephanie struggled with the reality of becoming a parent and maintaining a successful career and business. They welcomed their second child in 2019, and are now figuring out parenting with two children. Stephanie most recently opened a second business, which follows her ultimate passion, baking! Stephanie is not afraid to go after new adventures and face challenges; she believes it's what strengthens her as a woman and mother. Stephanie believes that all moms should do whatever it is they want in life and to follow their passions. Her ultimate goal is to be the best role model for her kids. Stephanie currently resides in the Muskoka area of Canada with her husband Ryan and their two children Bria and Cole.

It's Okay to Be Selfish, Mama

Have you ever been on a plane and as the flight attendant is giving you the safety presentation they say, "If you are travelling with a young person and there is a drastic change in pressure inside the cabin and your oxygen mask drops, place one on yourself first, and then your child"? Wait, what? They have got to be kidding. There is no way, no how I am letting my child suffer and not put one on them . . . wait a second. If I am not taken care of by putting my oxygen mask on, what good am I to my child? This has always been in the back of my mind when thinking of self-love and self-care. As moms I feel like we assume everyone is judging and even more so if we decide we want to get away for a night, get our hair or nails done. Are we being selfish? YES! Of course we are! But at the same time, NO, we aren't!

Growing up, I had the most incredible role model—my mom. She was a working mom for as long as I can remember. As a child, my dad stayed home while my mom worked and I didn't think it was strange because that's all I knew. It turns out she was a badass working mom! When I was in high school she put herself through university and she now has an incredible career. Thanks to her I had an amazing example of what a working mom can accomplish! As a kid my mom did everything for us kids. As far as I can remember, her taking time out of the day to do something for her just wasn't something she did. The needs of our family were always met. Now, as an adult and a mom, I love going with my mom for self-care: pedicures, shopping, etc., as that is something she never did for herself when we were young.

Before I had my kids and my marriage, I had my career. It was something that I could honestly say I was proud of. Working in a male dominated career for the government was a big accomplishment for me. Then something even bigger happened—I became a mom. It took me some time to realize this but guess what? It is possible to have both! IT IS POSSIBLE TO HAVE BOTH.

When I was due back to work after my first child, I *didn't* have all the nerves, emotions, and anxieties that I had heard other moms talk about. That made me think I was a terrible mom. I wanted to go back to work. I couldn't wait to get back to work—I loved my career. Was that wrong of a mother? After my maternity leave I went back to work after eleven months, why? To let my husband take the last six weeks home with the baby. Guess what? I wasn't that sad about it. Did it make me a selfish mom? At the time I thought it did. I wasn't sad that she was now home with her dad—I felt he needed time to bond with her just as much as I did. I wasn't sad that she was starting daycare soon. Did I miss her? Absolutely! Did I miss being home with her? Of course! BUT here is the thing—being a mom is my favorite JOB of all, but there is more to me than just being a mom! I am a wife, I have a career, and own a business—two in fact! Was it selfish to want to have it all? Some may think so. But I was determined to have it all and do it all. I enjoyed being back at work. I enjoyed the feeling I got from my daughter when she saw me after getting home from work. Was it hard, HELL yes it was hard! Was it worth it! Hell yes it was worth it!

When it came to balancing my relationship with my husband, being a mom, working full time, having an online global business—and can't forget about the dog—some days I felt like a hamster running on a wheel.

Being a working mom is so hard. Being a stay-at-home mom is so hard—you know what, just being a mom is hard work!

Now that I am on my second maternity leave, life has changed a little bit. Do I still consider myself a working mama, of course! Being a mom is work in itself! BUT I now have two businesses—one I run online and one I work from my home. My career is still there, but currently at the back of my mind. Now taking care of two small children (one is three years and one is ten months) that is my full time job! Let me tell you, for all the full-time stay-at home moms out there, kudos to you! For all those working full time plus raising kids, kudos to you! I realized that whatever you decide to do, IT'S OKAY! It is okay to want to go back to work and leave your kids at daycare. It is also okay to not want to go back to work and not want to leave them at daycare.

I decided that I wanted to combine the best of both worlds—raising my kids but also working, and the best way I could find to do that was to open another business. An in-home business where I could set my own hours and work, but still be near for the kids. Now it was just a matter of balancing everything the best way I knew how. By setting work hours it would make me available for my business and for my family. When the kids are in school or daycare, working on my home business; and when my family is at home, focus on family time. If and when I return to my full-time career, it will be managing my career working hours, my business hours, and family time. Having a family schedule is my biggest tip—almost as important as a work schedule.

I have found some incredible mom friends over the years, and something I have noticed is: as moms, it is so EASY to judge each other! Why is that? Why do we do that? Honestly, I am not sure why? Maybe some moms believe their way is the only way, but in theory doing what-ever works best for you is what you should do. Being a part of this book means working together with other moms, encouraging other moms, and just cheering each other on! How amazing right? Why can't we do this all time?

I remember when I was pregnant and I would go get a pedicure, go shopping, get my hair done, and people would make comments like, "Well you better get all that in now because once that baby arrives you won't get to do any of it." For the most part that advice was coming from fellow moms! I thought well OK I guess not, right? They are moms, they would know best! After my first baby arrived, I thought WHY couldn't I still do all those things? Was it frowned upon in the "mom world"?

Which then leads me to this quote I saw online:

"Want to be a good mother? Take care of yourself. Run. Cry. Go to therapy. Be alone. Take a bubble bath. Scream. Get a babysitter. Eat that cake. Quit guilt. Ride in your car with the radio blasting. Have a glass of wine. Get your nails done. Read. Whatever needs to be done, do it. You need to be OK. You got this girl." -Unknown

After reading this I thought, why don't more mom's feel this way? Why do we have it in our heads that we can't do all these things? Can't do all the things we want to do? I think as moms we are always under the impression that our needs don't matter, that our self-care doesn't matter. Well I am here to tell you they do. Do my needs come first? No, not really! But, I am focused on making sure my needs are also met. Realizing that I am not being selfish and knowing that a cared for mom is a productive mom.

After deciding on a chapter theme I reached out my sister Colette— an awesome rock-star mom of two; I asked her what her thoughts are on being a working mom and a selfish mom;

"My advice on being a working mom would be that it isn't easy but it's worth it. You get a chance to do what you're good at, while modeling what strong women can do! We can do it all. You've got to have good people around you who love and support you. My mom hack is to make sure to meal plan and cook a day ahead so that hungry screaming tiny humans don't become hangry."

When it comes to being selfish she says, "You can't be a good mom if you don't find things you love to do. So whether it's a run, or massage, or nails, it doesn't matter you have to find time to be you."

It was so amazing to hear her say this as too many times I have been told, read somewhere, or overheard from someone that it's selfish to make time for yourself.

It has taken me awhile to come to terms with this, but I now know, and I am sure my husband can agree, that taking time for myself has made a positive difference in my moods, and in my ability to understand, support, and be present for my family.

I wanted to briefly describe what a day for me as a working mama looks like while currently working from home and also on maternity leave. Our mornings start early as most moms do I'm sure. My husband gets himself ready and heads to work. My oldest goes to daycare three days a week so on those days my husband drops her off and picks her up. Then it's time to get breakfast ready and get everyone settled into their morning routine. I then check my schedule to see what I have on the go that day. Some days it's online meetings that I schedule around nap times, sometimes it's being in the kitchen all day baking away for multiple clients that week—owning a home based bakery sometimes means long days in the kitchen, but also means days off when I choose! Also in there, I have to figure out meal prep, getting groceries, running errands, finding the time to do some self-care (reading, working out etc.), and finding time to visit with friends when possible. Oh, and also making sure the baby is fed! When my husband gets home it's then getting dinner started, making sure everyone eats it, and catching up with him about his day and mine. Then it seems it's right into bath time and bedtime routines! How fast do the days seem to go by? Isn't it crazy? After all the craziness is over, I can reflect on the day. Some days are easy and other days I make it through on autopilot, but I know that I wouldn't change a thing. Following a routine with meal prepping and planning and having a schedule for the week is a huge help for our family!

After this maternity leave is over I don't know if I have the same passions I did before about returning to my career because of my two businesses, but I am still career focused and career driven. I want to show my kids it's possible to go after their goals and follow their dreams. Want to be a stay-at-home mom or dad? DO IT. Want to be a doctor? Do that too! Want to work in the trades—chase those dreams.

There are days when it isn't possible to sit down and do self-care, but I feel that during each week you HAVE to make time for yourself. Having a partner who knows and appreciates this is so important. Taking a break from your day as a mom to hit the gym, coffee with a friend, or just to have alone time is so important for your well-being. I always know how much better I feel when I do something for myself.

When my first child was six weeks old I left her for two nights—how many shocked faces are out there right now reading that? BUT I left her with . . . her DAD! He was just as much of a parent as I was . . . fifty-fifty.

We parent fifty-fifty as best we can! When she was only four weeks old, he left her for four nights—are as many people shocked by that? Why? Why do we have this perception that dads going away on fishing trips, golf trips, boys nights, are okay, but a mom wanting to do anything for herself is perceived as selfish. As moms we need to get out of our own heads, stop caring about what other people think and make ourselves a priority.

It's not selfish, it's smart!

Was there some unwritten rule that said as a mom I am no longer allowed to take care of myself? Honestly, I think there is. There is this stigma that moms are selfish and are bad moms if they want time away from their babies.

Well I am here to tell you, *IT'S OKAY to be selfish, mama*! I have learned over my four years of being a mom that I need to take care of myself. For some, you may feel you aren't ready to leave your baby. That's okay too! My advice for that is to find a place where you can get your hair done or get a pedicure where you can bring your baby. People love babies! My hairdresser Cristen is now a close friend and she looks forward to seeing my little one! But, I am also ok with asking for help to look after my kids if I need a break! YES, we need breaks and we deserve breaks!

Asking for help is ok. Asking your partner for help, your friends, your family, anyone you feel comfortable with, ASK!

"Self care is not selfish, or self indulgent. We cannot nurture from a dry well. We need to take care of our own needs first, then we can give from our surplus, our abundance."
—Jennifer Loudon, Author

If our well is dry, how can we serve others? If we are burning out at both ends, how can we survive? The answer is, we can't! My advice to you right now is go and book yourself a spa appointment—or whatever you love to do, and just do it! Make yourself a priority. You are a great mom, you are always taking care of others and it's time you looked in that mirror and take care of the person who most deserves it! YOU.

Chapter Nineteen

Single Mama's Can Work It All

"Divorce happened to me. It changed my life, it sent me back to the office, it put my dreams on hold, it made me a single mom. But it also gave me more drive, more determination, and that extra push I needed to become the mom and woman I knew I always wanted to be."

Erin Montgomery

ERIN MONTGOMERY

www.thewriterwithrednails.com
ig: @thewriterwithrednails
Goodreads: www.goodreads.com/thewriterwithrednails

Erin Montgomery

Erin is a journalism graduate with over ten years of writing experience. Over the years Erin has developed her skills to include, PR, social media advertising and marketing, media relations, and web design. Erin is also the editor and founder of *Flourish Magazine*, which is a quarterly magazine written for moms by moms. Flourish is all about real talk, no expert advice. Erin is also a single mom to three little ones and resides just outside of Hamilton, Ontario.

"How would you feel if I said I wanted to separate?" When my husband of eight years spoke those words to me, my immediate response was, "I would feel like I don't want to separate." He had already made up his mind. So there; I was a mom of three—one being just four months old—and a recent divorcee. And the last time I had a *regular* job was maybe five years prior to that. The question quickly went from *what happened to my marriage* to *how do I support three children on my own?*

If you were to ask me five years ago where I saw myself in the future, the answer wouldn't be *divorced*. But that is where I was. I had a business: I worked freelance and part-time, so I could be fully present for the little people who depended on me. I was a wife, a mom, a business owner, but maybe some things just weren't meant to last?

Divorce changed my life and while some, okay a lot, of those changes were difficult and tested me, divorce also gave me a fresh life. Divorce gave me determination, drive, and that extra push I needed. My divorce was unexpected and out of the blue, it was hard to grieve the loss of a marriage when I had to pick up and provide for three children. Over the last couple of years a common phrase I have heard is "you are so strong, you have done such a great job." But I didn't feel that way. Yes my marriage was over, yes I was a single mom, yes I had to go back to work, but I felt like I did what every mom in my situation would have done. They would have made it work because if they don't, who will?

"Mom, did you pack my lunch?"

"Mom, where is my dance bag?"

"Mom, are we going to your work after school?"

Show of hands—how many of you heard your own child's voice with those questions? I don't know how many times I have been asked the same questions, and the answers are always the same. I swear I sound like a broken record. Maybe I should record my voice and just play it in the morning, the kids will think I am answering them meanwhile I am enjoying a HOT coffee—isn't that the dream?

But in reality those questions are just part of our daily routine now. My life has shifted, my priorities are different, my work life is different. This is what divorce does. It causes shifts and unfamiliar experiences; it causes hard decisions and lots of multi-tasking. Five years ago I was a mom, a wife, a business owner, and now I am a working single mom to three little people.

After my divorce, my primary focus was finding a job. At that point in my life I knew I needed a more stable income, I needed benefits and a regular paycheque, and I needed security. While working for myself would have been a dream, which allowed me more face time with my kids, a steady income trumped that. At least for now.

Here is the thing about re-entering the workforce after a stint of not being there: it's downright hard and super judgmental. At least that was my experience.

Something I learned quickly was that no matter how well educated I was, how qualified I was, or how impeccably I dressed, the moment the words "I am a single mom" left my mouth, the tone in that interview changed. It's like being a single mom plagued me as someone who couldn't commit to working full time. No matter what employers and recruiters told me, as a single mom, I was a risk. And that *risk* translated into a lot of other areas in my life.

Securing a mortgage as a single mom with dependent children is incredibly difficult. No matter how great my credit score was, how much money I put down, or how much money I was making, the answer I got from most (if not every lender), was that I was a risk. Simply because I had dependent children and that I was not married. Some people still believe that if you are a mom, you can't be a great employee; that as a single mom you wouldn't be able to pay your bills; or that moms just can't do it all. But let me tell you, as a single mom—the sheer driving force I have to succeed is far greater than any recent graduate because, unlike them, I *have* to provide, I *need* to have security, and I have dependent children—and to me, that makes me an *ideal* candidate.

So there I was, thirty something years old, with two school-aged children and a little baby on my hip, hustling to get back into the corporate world, which I had tried so hard to leave behind. I spent a few months searching for a full-time job in close proximity to home and a little flexible; I emailed thousands of resumes, and I interviewed tirelessly. I was defeated. But as a single mom, I knew I couldn't answer to defeat, no matter how many times she came knocking on my door. I pushed through, and I did it. I landed a full-time job that allowed my littles to come to work with me after school to avoid after school daycare payments.

I made it work.

Going back to the corporate world after being absent for about three years was like starting at a new school. Those fears of, *will they like me, will I make friends, am I dressed okay, am I going to fall behind?* They were real, and they wouldn't go away. The first few weeks back at it were difficult, it was an adjustment period. We were adjusting to an alternative family life, and the kids were adjusting to me not being there all the time.

> *Thankfully kids are resilient, and we have been working through the transition from being home to going to work.*

But with my dreams on the back burner, they were still calling my name, and now the new challenge began. How do I, as a single working mom, show my kids that their dreams can be realities no matter what obstacles are put in front of them?

You start a side hustle, that's how!

"Are you crazy?" I know some of you may think, most everyone else thought it too. But I have always believed that there has to be more to life than just graduating, finding a career, and working forever. I had a marriage, though it failed, it taught me things about myself. I had children, I had a career, now I needed something for myself. Cue, the side hustle.

My side hustle gave me a creative outlet, an over encompassing sense of achievement, it allowed me to move my dreams from the back burner onto the front burner. That small side hustle of mine gave me my dreams back. And while at this moment I am not taking it full time and have no immediate plans to do so, it's made me feel like going back to work isn't all that bad.

I am sure you have a lot of questions about how to run a successful side hustle, excel in your career, and be the super mom all at the same time; and while I definitely don't have all the answers, I have found a few hacks that have helped manage it all and not lose sight of the reasons why I started in the first place: my kids.

GET A CALENDAR:

And I don't mean the Google calendar app on your phone, although I use that to, I mean a paper calendar, a planner, a spot you can quickly check each morning and each night to see what's happening and what's upcoming for the week. The written planner, that whole paper and pen idea, has really helped us map out our weekly schedules—and it's easy for the kids to read. Now, my calendar would probably cause your anxiety to spike, every day is jam-packed, and there is no free space, but it works for us. Our schedule matches up seamlessly, and somehow I can be present at every after school activity for every kid, I never miss a thing. And with three kids that is an accomplishment all on its own. That planner and those written pages were a game changer for this whole single mama juggling act I am trying to navigate. And yes, for all of you wondering, I totally schedule working time into the planner.

MEAL PREP:

Now I am not talking about pre-portioning food into containers for everyone for the week, but when I say "meal prep," I mean creating a menu. In our house we have a framed chalkboard on the wall with our weekly menu, the kids know what they are eating for the week, and it also gives them a chance to pick a special dinner item. This menu has cut down our grocery bill, and has made it easier to prepare dinner. I don't feel frazzled anymore, and more importantly, I can make dinner the night before so no one gets cranky while waiting for their dinner to cook. Cause let me tell you, ain't nothing worse than a two year old who hasn't eaten!

ALONE TIME:

While this one may not be a "hack" per say, it is one of (if not the only) ways I can keep my sanity as a single working mom. I am strict with bedtime at my house. All the kids (regardless of age) are in bed with doors closed by 7:30 p.m. Now whether they choose to sit up and read a book for thirty minutes, or go right to sleep, is up to them—but my "mom duties" end at 7:30 p.m. This allows me time to just be, to prep for the next morning, to catch up on reality TV, to read a book, or to simply have a shower. Now I realize a 7:30 p.m. bedtime may not be reasonable for every family, it works for us. Those moments of quiet are what I need after a long day of work, after extra-curricular activities, and after my taxi driving responsibilities, to just unwind and pause.

I am a single working mom and for the foreseeable future that isn't going to change. I have faced a lot of uphill battles as a working mom; I have had to call in sick when my child had a fever; I have had to leave earlier, so I can attend an awards ceremony or a mid-day science fair; I have also had to use vacation days to be present at dance competitions, but I wouldn't trade it for the world.

Being a single working mom is no walk in the park, but for me it is an opportunity to prove to myself, my kids, and everyone who said I couldn't do it all; that I can.

It takes a little patience, a lot of planning, and scheduling (a couple glasses of wine!), but I have made it, and I will continue to make it every day, every game, every competition, every doctor's appointment. I will be there.

Let me be completely and totally honest with you. I am tired. All the time. You might be reading this and thinking to yourself she has this all figured out, she has made it work, and she is excelling. But I'm not. I have figured out ways to help deal with some of the stresses that come with single motherhood, but I don't have it all figured out.

Being a working mom is a lot of pressure, there are a lot of expectations both at work and at home, and I am doing my best. I am keeping my head above water. And that's all I can do, and that is all any mother can do. Their best.

I hope what you take away from this chapter is that you are doing your best, that there is a mom somewhere out there that is in (or has been in) your shoes, who has experienced divorce, who has gone back to the corporate world, who has had their white picket fence removed. I want you to leave this chapter knowing that when circumstances change and life takes you in a different direction, that you can come out the other side. That you are stronger than you can ever imagine.

One of the paramount things I took away from my divorce was that no matter what curveballs life throws at you, you just have to be ready for them. Now, I am in no way recommending that you prepare for a divorce, but be ready for the possibility of having to go back to work at any point. I wasn't ready. I had lived in a bubble of marriage, thinking this was how my life would be for the next twenty years, but I quickly learned that sometimes life has other things in mind for you.

Life circumstances can change at any point and the best thing you can do for yourself and for your family is to just be as prepared as you possibly can. Keep up to date on your schooling, take an online course, work a freelance job. No matter how hard you plan your life and your white picket fence, sometimes it's just not meant to be. And that's ok, Mama!

Chapter twenty

Work it, Girl!

"Because I said so."—Mom

Sharlene Rochard

SHARLENE ROCHARD

www.sharlenerochard.com
ig: @sharlenerochardlund | fb: @sharlenerochard
li: @sharlenerochard

Sharlene Rochard

Sharlene Rochard Lund was born in Ontario, Canada to parents of Trinidad & Tobago and European descent. Sharlene knew exactly where she was going in life from a very early age. At the age of four she started performing in theater productions, at age thirteen she was Miss Pre-Teen Canada.

The launch of her professional modeling career soon followed. Sharlene became one of the most successful and sought-after models in Canada, featured in many campaigns and major magazines. By the age of seventeen she was travelling the world as a model.

After studying acting at the Neighborhood Playhouse in New York, and the Beverly Hills Playhouse in Los Angeles, she landed her first movie. Her filmography includes *The Little Richard Story* directed by Robert Townsend, and he has acted in many movies since.

Sharlene was born to perform and has been in the public eye since she was four. Her life has taught her many things, including how to be a working mom. Sharlene is the model mom who keeps on working no matter what life throws at her.

Work it, Girl!

If you read my other book chapter in *Fitness to Freedom*, then you have an idea of my story. If you have not, here is the short version. I'm a mom, model, actress, writer, and filmmaker. I had four kids in under three and a half years. How is that possible, you ask? I had twins, then two more, one right after the other. Was I crazy? Yes! Were they all supposed to be on this earth? Yes. Do I want to tear my hair out most of the time? Yes. The pregnancies were difficult, and all the kids came way too fast, meaning I wasn't ready to be a mom, like, ever. Nobody warns you about being a mom! Everyone says, "Congratulations!" like you won the lottery!

However, they should have said, "Congrats! You will probably never get a good night's sleep ever again. Your life will be changed forever, and it will not be easy. Enjoy!" Imagine if people told you the truth. Now when someone tells me they are going to have a baby, I seriously don't know what to say! My twins are nine now, and I have never slept through a whole night since before they were born. Even if I have had the luxury of staying in a hotel for a night, my internal clock wakes me up because I am so used to someone needing something in the middle of the night. "Mom, I can't sleep. Who is the sandman? Mom, can I have some water? Mom, can I sleep with you? Mom, Mom, Mom" . . . it never ends.

I was a top model. I was traveling the world. I was having a blast! My life rocked! Then wham-bam thank you, mam, I got pregnant with twins. At thirteen weeks, I was stuck in the hospital. I had complications, and the doctor said: "you're staying until these babies are born." Goodbye modeling while I was pregnant, goodbye getting any nursery ready before the babies came home. Goodbye, life. I was stuck in the hospital. I will spare you all the details of why I was stuck in the hospital for six months and how I got through it. Let's just say I survived, and I helped countless other women in the hospital. I say countless because I received the award for the earliest admission and longest stay in the pregnancy ward.

We are all survivors in our own right, and to all the ladies who have had (or are having) complicated pregnancies, the more power to you! You're amazing! You're doing it, and you will get through anything after this!

Work it, Girl!

There is nothing stronger than female willpower.

I loved my job, and I still love my job, but the last thing I needed as a model was to get pregnant for three-and-a-half years straight. My job depends on how I look. Yes, it can be superficial, but I'm not. I need to look good in front of the camera, but who doesn't want to look good, anyway? The question I faced was, "How am I going to get back to work? How can I lose this baby fat?"

All the details of how I lost the weight is in the book *Fitness to Freedom*, and this is about how I started working again.

Getting into physical shape was hard, but now I am modeling in magazines and campaigns again.

How did I do it?

First, I got into shape; not just my body but my mind. I was tired of changing smelly diapers all day and making all types of food mush. I had to get out of the post-baby blues and put my mind at ease. I had to realize that these four bundles of joy would be okay without me. A break, for everyone, is okay! I started first by leaving them with my mom, whom I trusted the most. The second hardest part was leaving them in the children's play area at the gym; I would work out and then pick them up after. If they needed anything, I was close by. Both situations went very well. At first, I had to learn to trust people and accept that the kids would be taken care of. I have no idea where this motherly instinct comes from, but all mothers have it, and I've heard it stays with you for life.

Third: "Audible," ladies! Audible is my best friend and savior. Audible, if you are reading this, I love you! You kept me sane during those witching hours. I have books on my phone. I wear headphones. Four screaming children all under the age of four. How the hell did I not go crazy? Books on my phone! I would put a book on, and go to another planet. Those kids could cry in my face, and I would just smile and nod. The kids were like, "Mommy, you are so nice." It's because I can't hear you! Self-help books are great and get you thinking of how fantastic life can be. When you are scrubbing the floor after breakfast, lunch, and dinner—because most of the food ends up on the floor, you can listen to your book and think of how amazing you are. The principal thing to focus on is your mind. You have to be a sound person to be a strong parent. Audible helped me achieve confidence and stay sane. Not only is Audible great for parents' sanity it's awesome for bedtime! When you are just way too tired for another book or any book at all download a book for kids like *Harry Potter* or anything age-appropriate, tuck them in, turn out the lights and have them listen to books on your phone. It's genius! They love it and it's a peaceful way to get them in bed. The tactics they use such as "I'm not tired, I'm hungry, I want a glass of water," don't last as long as they look forward to hearing the story.

Every working mom needs
audiobooks in their toolbox.

I wanted to be the best mother I could be. I felt like I was. I tried so hard to be that Pinterest Mom with the awesome-looking birthday parties. I thought that was what being a mother was all about. Ha! Was I wrong! Lots of people want to tell you what to do and how to do it. But once again, you know best, nobody has instincts for their child like the mother. Do what you want, how you want, and do it proudly. As I gained confidence in myself as a mother and others around me to help me with my children, I started to look outside of the house, and I realized I had a life before these kids came along and drove a train right through my house, life, and mind!

I just knew from the bottom of my heart that I should go back to work. Staying at home was just not me anymore. Cleaning up toys all day, the spit up, crap in my hair, wiping poop, sweatpants every day all day is amazing, but it just isn't me. There is no one in the world that says, "I'd like to clean forty diapers today, and put up with four screaming lunatics that don't care about me too much." It did not seem like they cared for me too much at times, anyway. They just want to sleep, eat, and play. They will smile and melt your heart, then ask for more. I also wanted more, however, more from my life. I was really unhappy about staying at home.

Praise to the full-time moms! You are working
twenty-four hours, seven days a week!

Going back to work is a break. These stay-at-home moms have their shit together. Those children run you around like you are their slave, and I decided I wasn't going to let a two-year-old run me around anymore. I was a working model who traveled everywhere long before kids, and I missed it a lot, so I called all my agencies and told them I was ready to work.

It was different, I must confess; I was different. My hips were a bit bigger, my boobs a bit more saggy, and I have a few more stress lines, but all in all, I'm a mom, and it is okay. The beauty industry is changing.

They want more real looking women, and I looked more real (whatever that means!). It's hard to go back to work. It is, but it just takes that first step to walk out the door, then trust me, you will run out the door as fast as you can some days.

The main thing is your mind. You have to know that your happiness makes your kids happy. Going to work is peaceful to me. I cannot go five seconds in my house without a "Mommy; I need, I'm hungry, Olivia hit me." Work is like going to the spa! Peace! It is amazing!

The fourth step I found hard was when I am working, what are these children going to eat? It is easy when they are babies; it is just a bottle. But as they grow into toddlers and school-aged kids, they need to eat real food. Welcome, easy-to-cook food! Mac and Cheese is a lifesaver! It might not be nutritious, but on the nights when I am exhausted and too tired to cook, it's a *mac and cheese* night! It is not the healthiest option, but they are not going to die if they have it every now and again.

Here is a tip: whenever you have time to cook some cauliflower, mash it up, blend it in a blender and divide it into ice cube trays, and add one cube to the mac and cheese you make out of the box. There, veggies are included, and you don't have to feel guilty! It's an easy and smart way to add vegetables, and nobody knows except you. Kids are happy, Mom is happy, and you are the coolest mom around! Try this with different vegetables and different dishes, you never know what will work for your family!

After I figured out that I could go back to work and everything was going to be okay, the fifth step for me was scheduling. Humans survive best on a daily schedule, and to prevent getting completely exhausted, I brain drain everything that needs to be done into my phone and onto the calendar on my fridge. When things overlap, my calendar tells me. If I know I will forget a doctor's appointment, I put an alarm on it. Calendars are like your own personal secretary. There is just too much to remember and I would forget just about everything without my calendars. They even make a special mom calendar with stickers your kids can steal from you! Here is the tricky part about this step that as a single mom of four I have figured out: schedule everything! Write out all of your to-do's, when you do your laundry, when you fold the laundry, get the car's oil changed, buy new shoes for kids dance classes, in the calendar and color code it. The kid's activities are one color, to do's are another.

When I started to micromanage myself I noticed how much happier I became. It is easy for a mom to second guess everything she does and not feel appreciated. The key is to appreciate yourself at all levels and realize that you don't have to be perfect. If you only get the laundry done because that was all you had time for, it is okay, and it is a checkmark on the *done* list for the day. Working and taking care of a family is hard. Anyone who says it is easy is lying. The struggle is real. Not only am I working right now, but I also went back to school, wrote a movie, directed and acted in it, all at the same time while taking care of four kids and writing this chapter!

Everyone asks me how I do it all. The answer is I have no idea except that I was tired of the constant state of *lost* and *confused*. With four kids around I can't think about anything but whatever they are saying, and honestly it doesn't make sense half the time. Last night my daughter said to me as she was listening to the audiobook I put on "Mom, can you back forward that part?" "What does that mean? Back forward is not a word and I don't understand what you are saying to me," I said. I kind of knew she wanted me to rewind the book, but if I lived in this "wordy-world" all day every day without work, I would go completely insane. Even my grocery list is on my phone because I have lost those little pieces of paper I put my list on, and forgot why I went to the grocery store in the first place.

The mom's brain is the real deal. Basically it means you forget everything except your baby. So write everything down and schedule it all, so you get everything done that you need to do.

Then feel good about every little thing because . . . why not?! You did it! No matter how small a task, it got done and nobody else is going to do it except you. Nobody knows your kids better than you. So strategize every day and stick to your plan.

Being a mom changes who you are and not always for the better. It can bring out the over-analyzer, over-controlling, over-anxious, over-cautious parts of you that you thought only existed "sometimes." Those feelings are here to stay in abundance until you can relax, and for me, the only place I get to relax is at work. It is so much easier to concentrate at work because nobody is asking me to wipe their bum every five seconds. Let's face it: having a baby is not easy, and moms juggle about a thousand things a day. It is the way our brain works. Men can only handle one thing at a time. Have you ever asked a man to do more than one thing at once like grocery shopping, or to go to the bathroom and not use the decoration towels you put there for show? In my experience, they always come back with a few things missing from your shopping list and they always use the towels you asked them not to use! Moms were made to handle tasks, lots of them!

Work it, Girl!

So going back to work after a baby is easy. No matter what happens you can handle anything!

If you can wake up every two hours to feed someone, cook, clean, and do laundry, girl, you're a Superhero! No matter what life throws at any mom she can figure it out.

Moms are strong and resilient. Let's face it, you gave birth to another human being! There is nothing more complicated than being a mom, and all the tasks you do that nobody sees. So when it is time to go to work, there is nobody better to hire than another mom.

Child care might not be cheap, and you might not be making much money at first, but your sanity is worth more. I would go to work for free. It's a break; it's fun. It's the best feeling in the world. I love my kids, but this mama's gotta work!

Acknowledgments

"To the love of my life Daniel Colosi, thank you for committing to this conscious parenting journey, and for choosing me EVERY. SINGLE. DAY. I dedicate this chapter to Aliyah & Luca."

-Marcia Miatke

"With heartfelt thanks to Sonya Degner. This amazing lady has dedicated her life to caring for the children of mama's who had to work. I am forever grateful for her kindness, support, and friendship."

-Sharon Hughes-Geekie

"My inspiration, the many children that have shared my path. Thank you Leo, Darcy, and Joe for allowing my inner mama bear to shine. Thank you Ashley for sharing Reese's birth and making me a godmother."

-Sally Lovelock

"To my Mama and Lola for paving my path so I can share this story and help others help themselves. To my why's—my husband and son—for loving me the way you do. My heart is complete."

-Mary Ann Masesar Blair

"To the mamas in this book, Catherine, Ky-Lee and GBRPH, my mama, and all the moms in my life for your wisdom. To DJ for supporting my dreams. To my whole world—Jax and Lil—for hiring me to play the best role I've ever had."

-Krysta Lee

"To my three great loves; Samantha, Liliana, and Marcus. My mamma here on earth and papa up in heaven. My amazing family and friends (including Sandra Carusi) for their love and support ♥."

-Pina Crispo

Acknowledgments

"My rock and love of my life, Ryan. There's no one I'd rather steer this ship with. Kiddo's, I love you to the moon and back. You drive me bonkers, but I'm proud of who you're becoming. Keep being you!"

-Amanda Drexler

"To my beautiful baby boy, Nathan, you're the greatest gift. You inspire and encourage me to be a better mama and businesswoman. To my husband for supporting me through this crazy journey."

-Lisa Evans

"To my soul sister, Krysta, for your beautiful idea and for asking me to share in it. To Rowan and Arion, I wouldn't be doing the work I am, and certainly wouldn't be a working mom without you."

-Elizabeth Meekes

"Thank you to my husband Mike and daughter Carson for all your love and support."

-Michelle Emmick

"To my daughters Ariana, Sofia, and Chiara. You're beautiful inside and out. To the love of my life, Jason, your strength is a crucial ingredient to me being the best version of myself."

-Teresa Nocita

"Thank you to my husband Anthony for always pushing me past my limit, my daughter Scarlett who made me a mother, and Harrison my son; when you were born, so was I."

-Domenica Orlando

"To GBR Publishing for the opportunity to be part of this book, and to Krysta Lee. To my son, Jack. To my own mother, who showed me what it looked like to be a strong, working mama."

-Melissa Killeleagh

"To GBR Publishing for making this happen, Andy and Kristen for helping me tell my story, and to my children, family, and friends who encourage and support me in times of sickness and health—love you all."

-Andie Mack

"To the wonderful team for putting this book together. To my hero, my father; he always encouraged me to do my best. To my youngest sons, Joseph and Rico, who are my daily inspiration to keep going."

-Nanci Lozano

"To Jonathan for forgiving me for tossing and turning all night, encouraging me to travel and work, and for believing in me when my ego (often) gets in my way. I see you, I appreciate you, I love you."

-Charleyne Oulton

"Thank you to GBR publishing and their team. My husband and our army of kids, I love you all. My parents for always supporting me, and to Jesus for being good, all the time."

-Laura Morris

"Thank you to my mom for being an incredible role model as a working mom, and my husband Ryan for being my biggest fan and supporter."

-Stephanie Card

"To my kids. Without them I don't know where I'd be; with them I know I have accomplished something amazing. Thank you for making me a mom and always keeping me on my toes."

-Erin Montgomery

"To my kids, Trent, Bella, Olivia, and Liam Lund. Being your mom has been the best gift of all. To my mom for showing me how to be a working mom. I learned from the best!"

-Sharlene Rochard

Epilogue

As the days, months, and years go by, you too may find yourself repeating the words *Mama's Gotta Work* to your minis. Some days that phrase may be followed by "... *darling.*" Other days, it might end with " ... *dammit!!*" Either way it's ok—*we're all doing it.* Somewhere out there we're journeying through the same storm on a different boat, sailing the seas alongside you, mama!

There are no problems, pains, or powers (nor even a *pandemic*, apparently!) that could ever completely stop a mama's *GO!* All mothers are *always* working, and with that signature mama-bear drive and determination (and drinks of her choice), moms always prevail inevitably.

The hustle may be full on at times, and other times it might feel like an easy-breezy *grow-with-it* flow. Whatever the way, on whatever the day, it's *all* good. Your experiences are shaping your unique story, and you're leading by example—this is inspiring others along the way! No matter what anyone else thinks, you're not *just* a working mom, and you can never be defined by *or confined to* any permanent title.

*Remember: you don't have to do what every other mom is doing; **your best is enough.***

Remind yourself often that *you're enough,* too. Sometimes the hardest person to love is our self, especially when feeling lost between kids and careers, as moms who work do. You are worthy of everything your big-and-beautiful mama heart desires, and you deserve all the grandest things in life! Learn to love yourself as you love your children *unconditionally*, because ironically, that's the greatest gift you could ever give to your family.

Day by day, in many ways, mamas become stronger, wiser, and more resilient with practice. As we fail forward, we move one step closer to a brighter future for working mamas. Ultimately this includes a greater level of conscious parenting, an abundance of success within our careers, and the truest fulfillments our sweetest dreams can imagine!

Epilogue

*May we come together in pieces,
and work together in peace . . . and quiet
. . . sweet, sweet, quiet.*

Please feel free to communicate, collaborate, and congratulate all working mamas along with us, and among your individual mama-tribes too! What works for one may not work for us all, however life can be so much better when we work together. Keep an eye out for other moms who may be juggling along their journey, and offer a helping hand whenever possible. You never know the difference a small act of mindness can make, especially for the mamas who *gotta* work.

* * *

Lastly, on the days when it feels like World War Twenty-*thousand*: remember to breathe; keep your eyes on your *whys;* and most importantly of all . . .

*frame **this** baby and hang it on the wall:*

MAMA'S GOTTA WORK!

Entry is Strictly Prohibited!
The ONLY Acceptable Interruptions Are As Follows:

- You're on fire.

- Somebody else is on fire.

- Everything is on fire . . . and it's *not* raining.

- The cast of *Workin' Moms* is out back . . .
  reenacting scenes from Season 3, Episode 8.

- You broke a bone.

- Somebody else broke a bone.

- The dog broke a bone
  (. . . the dog broke its *actual* bone).

- One of us won the lottery . . .
  and there's a private jet waiting out front.

- You're choking.

- Somebody else is choking.

- The cat is choking
  (. . . hairballs do **not** qualify as choking).

- Michael Jackson came back to life . . .
  and he is performing *Thriller*.

- You're dying.

- Somebody else is dying.

- There's an apocalypse . . . and everyone is dying.

- The E.T.'s are here . . .
  and want to come inside.

- You broke into mama's ***special*** cabinet.

- Somebody else broke into mama's ***special*** cabinet.

- Mama broke into mama's ***special*** cabinet.

- Or . . . there's a life and death situation . . . involving
  your father.

(Rules subject to change. Some restrictions may apply.)

END OF AVAILABLE OPTIONS

Love, Mom.

Just do what you *gotta* do,
and work it 'til it works,
beautiful mama!

Until next time . . .

- Krysta Lee xox

Check out some of our other titles

www.goldenbrickroad.pub
Shop at 20% off with promo code GOLD20

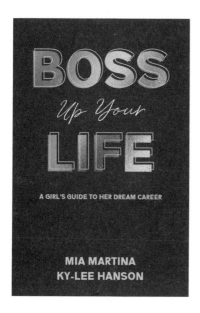

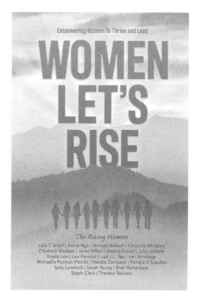

Check out some of our other titles

www.goldenbrickroad.pub
Shop at 20% off with promo code GOLD20

GOLDEN BRICK ROAD
PUBLISHING HOUSE

Link arms with us as we pave new paths to a better and more expansive world.

Golden Brick Road Publishing House (GBRPH) is a small, independently initiated boutique press created to provide social-innovation entrepreneurs, experts, and leaders a space in which they can develop their writing skills and content to reach existing audiences as well as new readers.

Serving an ambitious catalogue of books by individual authors, GBRPH also boasts a unique co-author program that capitalizes on the concept of "many hands make light work." GBRPH works with our authors as partners. Thanks to the value, originality, and fresh ideas we provide our readers, GBRPH books have won ten awards and are available in bookstores across North America.

We aim to develop content that effects positive social change while empowering and educating our members to help them strengthen themselves and the services they provide to their clients.

Iconoclastic, ambitious, and set to enable social innovation, GBRPH is helping our writers/partners make cultural change one book at a time.

Inquire today at www.goldenbrickroad.pub